WATERS FAR AND NEAR

Also by Charles Gaines

Fiction
Stay Hungry
Dangler
Survival Games

Nonfiction
Pumping Iron
Pumping Iron II: The Unprecedented Woman
Yours in Perfect Manhood: Charles Atlas
Staying Hard
A Family Place
The Next Valley Over: An Angler's Progress

WATERS FAR AND NEAR

Tales of Angling Adventure and Misadventure around the World

Charles Gaines

Guilford, Connecticut

An imprint of Rowman & Littlefield

Distributed by NATIONAL BOOK NETWORK

Copyright © 2015 by Charles Gaines
Illustrations by John Swan

"Rivers Owned in the Mind" originally published in *Astream: American Writers on Fly Fishing*, edited by Robert DeMott, Skyhorse Publishing © 2012.

British Library Cataloguing in Publication Information Available

Library of Congress Cataloging-in-Publication Data
Gaines, Charles, 1942–.
Waters far and near : tales of angling adventure and misadventure around the world / Charles Gaines.
pages cm.
ISBN 978-1-4930-0972-5 (hardcover)
1. Fishing—Anecdotes. 2. Gaines, Charles, 1942—Travel. I. Title.
SH441.G335 2015
799.12—dc23
2014041286

♾ ™ The paper used in this publication meets the minimum requirements of American National Standard for Information Sciences Permanence of Paper for Printed Library Materials, ANSI/NISO Z39.48-1992.

Printed in the United States of America

TO TOOTS
Who knew all about it

"If the angler take fysshe surely thenne is noo man merrier in his spryte."

—Dame Juliana Berners

Fhuair e air falbh.
(Gaelic for "It got away.")

CONTENTS

.

I

THE HAPPIEST MAN IN RUSSIA

At 5:30 a.m. in the Helsinki airport, it appeared the whole world had been reduced to well-fed men carrying rod cases. Standing in the endless, snaking line in front of the Finnair counter were Brits in their tweed jackets and Barbours, merry Spaniards, a dour group of French with belly-wallets and B.O., and pink-jowled Americans in checked Orvis shirts, boat shoes, and khakis.

There was also a lone Japanese, a stocky, smiling man carrying a rod case the size of a SAM launcher. "Where you coming from?" he asked me.

"Canada."

"Ahhh. Restigouche; Gaspé Peninsula. I fish Canada four times. Norway, two times. Iceland, six times. Where you go in Russia?"

"The Kharlovka, Litza, and Rynda," I told him. "And you?"

"Umba. Then I go Kharlovka. I fish there four times. Rynda too. You fish in salt water? This year already I been to Cuba, Solomon Islands, Belize, Guam . . ."

Guam? Now, I myself have spent a lunatic amount of time running around the world in order to interfere with the eating habits of pea-brained creatures with fins, but Guam was somehow over the top. "My God, man," I thundered. "Don't you do anything but fish?"

He considered. "Travel to get there."

When Rip and Hakan and I finally filed into our overstuffed plane, as dense with CEOs and investment bankers as the Knickerbocker Club, my Japanese friend was sipping champagne, the only passenger in first class. I couldn't help myself. "So what is Guam like?"

"Very big bonefish in Guam." He grinned. "But nothing like this. This is Holy Grail."

Quite, I was moved to think a few hours later in the helicopter. The Holy Grail: quite, as the Brits are forever saying. As it happened, I had just been told by an amiable English physician with a bottle of single malt Scotch peeking out of his backpack that last year a helicopter much like the one we were in had crashed into the unimaginable desolation presently below us.

"No one was killed. But they were on a riverbank for twelve hours without medical assistance, I'm afraid. It makes one think," said the doc.

This was after three hours in the airport at Helsinki, a two-hour flight over the bald emptiness of Lapland, three hours in the passport control line at Murmansk under the sour gaze of baby-faced Russian soldiers, followed by two or three more hours in the airport bar, drinking beer and watching Ozzy Osbourne sing in dubbed Russian on a black and white TV. Now sixteen or so of us were sitting with plugged ears on the bench seats of a rattling old MI-8 chopper with duct tape holding things together and wires hanging from the ceiling, flying over a roadless landscape of snow-patched tundra, glacial tarns, and a few pitifully stunted trees like . . . well, now that I thought about it, perhaps a bit like knights—steeled to task against all trepidation and tribulation, holding one shining purpose in mind.

"Quite," I told myself.

Russia's Kola Peninsula is a forty-thousand-square-mile thumb of ancient land pointing eastward from the junction of Finland, Sweden, Norway, and Russia, lying on the same latitude as Iceland, some 250 miles above the Arctic Circle. During the Cold War it was one of the most militarized places on earth. Now all those shivering Russian troops are gone, and the peninsula is inhabited again only by wolves, brown bears, Arctic foxes, reindeer, a few nomadic Saami Indians, and, from the first of June until mid-September, weekly flocks of international Atlantic salmon sports who pay up to $10,000 to sleep for seven nights in a tent or hut and stand waist-deep all day in a freezing river, believing all the time they are blessed beyond telling to do so.

As yet unruined by the commercial fishing, logging, damming, pesticides, aquaculture, and other scourges that have all but wiped out Atlantic salmon in the United States and most of Europe, the rivers of the Kola deliver not only what is arguably the world's best salmon fishing, but—even more precious, the Grail within the Grail, as it were—salmon fishing as it was primordially found: on wild, remote, utterly uncompromised rivers. Yokanga, Varzuga, Umba, Ponoi are a few of their mellifluous names. Some flow north into the Barents Sea, some south to the White Sea. Some are renowned for large numbers of small to medium-sized salmon: On these it is possible to catch more fish in a day than you could on most of the world's other premier salmon rivers in a week, and more in a week than many dedicated salmon fishers catch in a lifetime. I have an acquaintance who personally released 182 grilse (small salmon) and salmon in six and a half days on one of these rivers, and this more or less nonstop action is what most American anglers go to the Kola to find. But others are there on an entirely different quest, one of the most challenging in all of sport fishing, and it is for those discriminating few that an Englishman named Peter Power is in the happy and determined business of Grail acquisition. Let's say that you, like the Swedes, have refined down what you care about in salmon fishing to the occasion to catch big fish, "serious fish," by wading only, in situations demanding enough to sear each experience so permanently into your senses that years later you will still twitch like a sleeping bird dog to recall it. In that case, my friend, the Kharlovka, the Litza, and the Rynda—the three "northern rivers" of the Kola controlled by Power's company—are your true Holy Land.

I happen to have a taste for eccentric people, particularly those of a bighearted and voluble stripe, and I liked Peter Power immensely from the moment he greeted the helicopter, dressed in waders and a fishing jacket, greedily smoking a cigarette and shaking hands with each of us as we exited the chopper into a bright blue, high-latitude afternoon, with his splendid camp and then the river, looking cold, sharp, and glamorous as a saber blade, lying below us. About half of our group, friends of Peter's, were staying on there at Rynda; the rest of us were choppering on to the Kharlovka camp as soon as Peter had shown us around this one. After we had visited the main building with its inviting bar area and dining room, the sauna, the comfortable, single-person cabin units, and finally Peter's luxurious dacha, after we had gazed down from its deck to the river's creamy, frothing fall into the long, tea-colored glide of Home Pool, and then to its progress down the lovely Rynda Valley, pooling and shelving and running like God's own diagram of a salmon river, those of us who were leaving couldn't help but feel a bit . . . bereft.

"Not to worry," Peter told Rip and me. "We'll bring you two and Hakan and Per back here toward the end of the week for a couple of days. But Rynda is really dead men's shoes, don't you see?"

Well, no; but Rip and I followed Peter silently back inside the dacha, where he introduced us to his maid-servant, Nina—a gorgeous Apache-looking creature, wearing a red bandanna on her head and her long crow's-wing hair in pigtails—and then led us into his bedroom. "I can lie here in my bed," he said, proceeding to do so, "and watch a thousand reindeer cross in front of me. Who else can say that? I have fished fifty-four salmon rivers, and I have never seen a more perfect site for a house than this one. That chair there came from my cabin on the Laerdal. Oh, life. It's good fun, isn't it?"

He lit another in a constant progression of cigarettes and seemed to ponder the question. He was maybe six feet four inches tall, with great round, intelligent eyes behind thick glasses—a sixty-two-year-old recovered alcoholic and ex-merchant prince of considerable fortune, I had heard, with rather more than his model's normal miles on him and yet winningly boyish. "Well, you're off to Kharlovka," he said, popping up from the bed. "Did you know we have already taken nine fish over thirty pounds in the two weeks we've been open? And each one memorable. I don't believe anyone should be allowed more thirty-pound salmon or beautiful women than he can remember, do you?"

"Peter's a very interesting man," I said to his Swedish friend and fishing consultant, Per Stadigh, when we were back inside the helicopter.

"Quite complicated," said Per.

I wanted to ask him what dead men's shoes were but decided to wait and ask Peter at the end of the week.

In addition to Per, myself, and my friend Rip Cunningham, our group at Camp Kharlovka consisted of Swedish photographer Hakan Stenlund, Gilbert, the English doctor, and two young American fish hawks—Ken, the owner of a fly shop and a sporting booking agency in Oregon, and his buddy Brian, a pregnancy-complication physician. The camp was roomy and comfortable, if not as posh as Rynda, and impeccably run by its manager and Peter Power's overall director of operations, Volodya Kulagin.

Breakfast is at eight. At nine, you, your fishing partner, and your guide for the day are helicoptered off to one of six beats along the Kharlovka and the nearby Litza, where literally miles of river are yours alone for the day. You lunch heartily on the riverbank, and are choppered back to the camp at seven, in time for a sauna, shower, and a beverage or two from the amply supplied bar before an astonishingly good multicourse dinner at eight. Fishing in Kharlovka's Home Pool is open to you before breakfast, or after dinner *until* breakfast if you like, since it never gets any darker in the summer at this latitude than it is at four o'clock in the afternoon. If you are there, as we were, in late June or very early July—the prime time for big fish—you can quite comfortably expect the exacting, memory-seizing conditions that, one hopes, you are questing for: weather that can go in moments from practically Caribbean to a foggy, bone-chilling howl off the Barents Sea, and a very good chance of high water. In these northern Kola rivers, carved through volcanic tundra rock into hairy sequences of canyons and falls, high water often means long casts with sinking lines or "heads"; and it always means wading that is more or less the equivalent of a triple black diamond ski slope—wading that will likely not be at all your cup of tea if you are unfit, timid, or infirm.

Sliding a bit, with twice-replaced hips, into the latter two of those conditions, I nevertheless reckoned I was well-enough armed and armored for the joust. Rip, Per, Haken, and I, along

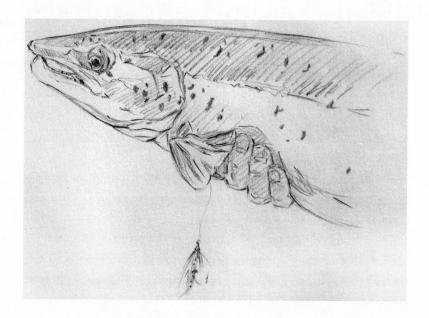

with our guide, Volodya, and a young fisheries scientist, had been choppered downriver to Rock Pool on our fist morning out. The water was only moderately high and the pool not very wide, so I loaded up a single-handed eight-weight rod with an intermediate sink-tip line and a black tube fly and sallied forth, wading out to hip depth over what felt to my suddenly alarmed feet like greased watermelons. There I stopped, feeling the current's startling grip and pull. A quickening north wind had begun to surround us with a cold fog blown in off the sea, less than a mile away; a salmon jumped near the tail of the pool, leaving a twenty-pound hole in the water; and suddenly through the fog I got my first glimpse of the real Kharlovka: an attack dog on uncertain leash. As I stood there waiting for the return of enough testosterone to carry on, I admit to feeling a surge of relief on remembering that two of my camp mates were physicians.

But one adjusts. Within a half hour I had caught my first Russian salmon, a dime-bright hen of twelve and a half pounds that was weighed and released by the fisheries scientist after he had fitted it with a tiny telemetry device by which the salmon's movements could be tracked over the summer. He opened his logbook and asked me to name the fish. I told him to call it Patricia, after my wife, and not to be too surprised if it turned up in whatever shoe stores there might be in Murmansk.

By lunchtime I had released two more salmon and we sat in a cold drizzle on boulders and ate soup, pastry-covered hot dogs and chocolate. A stoat, a weasly-looking thing with a long tail, chattered at us for handouts; a gyrfalcon soared above the river, which was a sullen silver, muscular and imperious, giving off like a breath the same promise of great and intricate pleasure mingled with the possibility of calamity that I remembered from decades ago at the bottom of certain ice climbs. Studying it, I felt a still-familiar quickening of senses, an eye-widening adrenal pop of qui vive that lingered with me throughout the week and came in particularly handy the next day on the Litza.

A fifteen-minute chopper flight east of Kharlovka, the Litza is eight kilometers (from the sea to a spectacular and impassable waterfall) of unforgiving plunge pools and bouldery runs—a paranoid young gunslinger with hopped up eyes, who will put a bullet in you over the color of your hat. Or so I fancied, perhaps overheatedly, as I trudged along a thin trail above the Litza gorge in weather out of *Wuthering Heights*, having just stood casting for hours on slippery footholds in a granite cliff twenty feet above Waterfall Pool, cajoling my aging balance in a cold mist created by the hissing thunder of the falls. At the bottom of the gorge—one missed step and a long fall to my right—a foaming, no-hope maelstrom seemed to grin up at me, gap-toothed.

Vassily—who also grins at you gap-toothed with two gold front teeth—is the Litza's antipoaching warden and tent-camp keeper. He lives on the river's bank throughout the season, alone except for two bear dogs. At fifty-five, he is rugged and direct as a crowbar, with meaty shoulders, assessing eyes, and hands like lobster claws. He sleeps with a Kalashnikov under his cot, with which he has killed twelve brown bears, if no poachers yet. We were Vassily's first overnight guests of the season and he did not need English to get across his hospitality. He slapped down a bottle of vodka and some little shot glasses onto the picnic table, and, for our entertainment, picked up a twenty-four-kilo dumbbell using only his little finger, and pressed it ten times overhead. As an encore, he did it again with the other hand. Then, grinning like the Litza, he went inside the cook tent and made us a supper of fried reindeer steak and boiled potatoes.

That night I slept long and well in a tent by the river while Rip and Per caught six salmon between them after midnight. The Litza's white noise put me back to sleep whenever I woke, and when I walked down to its bank under a cloudless sky for my morning wash, I found that we had somehow come to terms overnight. I often talk to rivers, and availing myself of our new chumminess, I mentioned to the Litza that I wouldn't at all mind a bit of sport this morning with one of its untrivial fish. I knew, for example, that a forty-four pounder had been caught here last year, and a thirty-nine pounder so far this season. Something along those lines was what I had in my mind, my own Grail salmon being a bright, well-shaped hen of forty pounds to the ounce.

Who can say rivers don't listen? A few hours later I was waist-deep in Snowbank Pool, swinging a fly upstream of a boulder into a lie I *knew* held my shining cup, the answer to tens of thousands of faithful questions cast and mended into scores of salmon rivers over dozens of years. The moment seemed exquisitely right.

Above me two honey buzzards and a sea eagle rode the bright air, fish were broaching everywhere, and it was absolutely impossible to think beyond where I was and what I was doing—a fair definition of time standing still. For no better reason than that I was in the hubristic mood to do it, I was fishing ridiculously undergunned, with a single-handed eight-weight rod, a floating line, and a small tube fly. Thus far that concatenation had yielded only two brown trout, fish I was thrilled with—full-figured, vividly colored native trout of eighteen to twenty inches—but that earned no more than disappointed shrugs from my guide, Volodya, who was seated on the bank above me. Then on my fourth or fifth swing through this lie of lies, on an upstream-mended, slower line, a fish took quietly, shook its head on the strike, and slouched downstream. When it stopped, forty yards away, I tightened down the drag on twenty-pound tippet, and it was like pulling on a rock.

I heard Volodya scrambling down the bank shouting something rapidly, maybe in English, and then the largest salmon I have ever hooked, my *very fish*, forty pounds or over, was pinned against the air at Michael Jordan altitude, and for a second Grace fell from the sky like silver rain. Then with a single contemptuous hurl of its head, the salmon tossed my little barbless Sunray Shadow halfway back to me. As I reeled in to Volodya's moans, the Litza grinned and spat a wad of Copenhagen. But I had seen what I had come to this place to see, and was as happy as a man could be.

Eight years ago, having quit drinking and having sold the plastic-strapping company that had made him "ridiculously successful," Peter Power began to look around for somewhere other than business and booze to apply his prodigious energy. He created a twenty-five-acre waterfowl park at his estate in Oxfordshire; he fished compulsively on all the great salmon rivers, including the

Rynda; and then, in 1997, when the camps on the Rynda and the Kharlovka came up for sale, he bought them, leased the million and a half acres surrounding them, and set out to do nothing less than develop the world's finest salmon-fishing destination. The biggest obstacle to that goal was poaching, which in 1997 accounted for fully half the fish taken from most of the Kola's rivers. Peter hired wardens (some of them ex-poachers), and now twelve of these, including the redoubtable Vassily—trained, armed with automatic weapons and radios, and guarding his rivers from ice out in May until freeze up in November—have all but eliminated the poaching. In just four years this program has almost achieved Peter's ambition for his rivers. In 2002, 227 rods caught 3,420 salmon there—for an average of fifteen fish per rod, more than double the number in 2000—at an average weight of fourteen pounds. Fifty of those fish were over thirty pounds, and five over forty. In the world of Atlantic salmon fishing that is simply Best in Show.

But great fishing destinations are inevitably something more than the numbers and sizes of the fish caught at them. In the case of Northern Rivers, that something has to do with the very nearly flawless day-to-day management of things that Peter gets from his huge, almost entirely Russian staff of sixty-nine (a ratio to guests of two to one), and to the pride those Russians take in their work. It has to do also, of course, with the millions of pounds Peter has thrown into his effort and the fact that he is, as he puts it, "above profit"; and, as much, with the fact that he is the only owner-operator on the Kola to live at his camp throughout the season. But more than anything, one surmises after spending only a little time with him, it has to do with the fact that all this is being done by the self-described "happiest man in Russia."

And why wouldn't he be? I had cause to wonder over the two days I spent with him at Rynda. Dead men's shoes, I learned, meant that the camp is run as a sort of private club, open only to people whom Peter invites, "people of kindred spirits," who do not pay to be there but rather make a contribution toward the common weal—people of the right sporting stuff. "It is civilized behavior that one is expected to bring here," Peter says. "There are no road signs. It is just what one *chooses* to do that counts."

On our first evening at the camp it was abundantly clear that one thing Peter chooses to do is ensure that his kindred spirits do not go hungry or thirsty. We began with single malt Scotch and canapés, went to king crab and champagne, then on to bottles of wine and vodka, a squid salad, two ducks carved at the table, Russian dumplings stuffed with meat, a banana flan . . . After dinner there were postcoital-like smiles on every angler's face and, unsurprisingly, a conversation arose on the relative glories of sex and salmon fishing. "Salmon fishing wins every time," was our host's summary comment. "One tends to forget the sex, but you remember every salmon."

The salmon and the fishing for them at Rynda camp were, in fact, particularly unforgettable. At Kharlovka I had asked the well-traveled Per Stadigh to enumerate for me the characteristics of his ideal salmon river and then to name which river in the world came closest to being that. "The Rynda" he had said without hesitation. And indeed, it is a very easy river to fall for—narrower and softer than the other two, more beautiful to my taste and more feminine, as challenging yet sweet-tempered as the perfect wife, and indulgent to those, like Rip, whom it chooses to favor. On our first day there, Rip had five fish; and on our second, ones of twenty-eight, twenty-six, and twenty-three pounds from Rock Island and Home Pools, while Peter showed Hakan and me the upper river and Lake Rynda by chopper, and indulged me at the lake in an hour or two of sampling what is without question one of the world's finest and least exploited brown trout fisheries. On dries and nymphs

Hakan and I took browns up to six pounds (they have been caught here to thirteen)—beautiful fish with daffodil-colored bellies and vivid black and red aureoles, many of them as given to taking to the air as salmon.

From Lake Rynda we choppered over to the Zolotaya, a winsome small salmon river, no more than thirty or forty feet across in places with lapidary pools and a spiffy new tent camp on its bank for overnight stays. Mikhair, the camp manager and warden, fed us lunch, then Peter and I sat talking and watching Hakan hook, play, and lose two large fish in Russian Pool. It was showery, with shafts of sun occasionally falling through the rain onto the pool, one of the most fetching I have ever encountered, and I would not have been at all surprised to see a mail glove rise from it holding a chalice.

On our last day at Rynda, Peter invited Rip and me up to his dacha for lunch and a chat. While being served prawn cocktails and pork chops by the lovely and mysterious Nina, I told Peter about my happiness with the great fish at Snowbank. Then I told him about the happiness I had the following day, our last at Kharlovka camp, in catching three salmon in two hours, one well over twenty pounds, from that river's stunning and daunting Waterfall Pool; and equally in watching his "fishing guru," the buoyant and sweet-natured salmon genius Per Stadigh, stand on a tiny ledge in the rock cliff across from me, handling his sixteen-foot double-handed rod with a finesse and precision that bordered on the magical.

"*Splendid*," said Peter. "I'd say then that you shortened your life a bit. I have a theory that the happier you are, the faster your life is. And by that standard I very well may be gone tomorrow. Quite simply, I am the happiest man in Russia." He grinned hugely and poured me some more wine. "If you had said to me eight years ago, 'Okay, Peter, I am going to give you all you want for the rest of your life,' I could not have asked for *anything* that would have given me one-third the joy of what I have now."

As we stood up from lunch to proceed to the afternoon's angling, Peter said, "I started life as one of the most predatory creatures alive. Like one of those nightmare Americans who always wants the best cabin, the most fish. All my life I've wanted things and used people—I was the worst of the type, the type I now have to either tame or blacklist from Rynda. But one learns that a bad life is advancing yourself at the expense of others, and that a good life is when you advance yourself and take other people with you."

He walked to a table where Nina had laid out for him three packages of cigarettes and three lighters, a number of handkerchiefs, his movie camera, and sunglasses. After she deposited these things into various of his pockets, he walked out to his entry deck, overlooking the Rynda's home pool, where Sergei, an ex-poacher who is now his man-servant and personal ghillie, helped him into his waders, fishing vest, and rain jacket.

"My God, isn't it *marvelous*?" Peter exclaimed, opening his arms as if to embrace all 1.5 million acres of his "private fiefdom." "No Scottish *Laird* ever had it better!" He turned to Rip and me, grinning again. "You see, I consider myself to be in the business of providing happiness, and how can I go wrong with all this as my stock-in-trade? I've done some great things in my life, but this is what I'd like to be remembered for: as the man who has created all this happiness." He lit a cigarette and pondered the great Grail river below us.

"Perhaps what Hugh Hefner was to girls," he said, "I may be to fishing."

2

A UNIVERSITY OF BONES

Just after noon the fishing shut down on the full tide as if someone had thrown a switch. Tom Montgomery and I and our guide, Donald Loze, waded the huge flat back to the skiff, which Donald steered through a maze of channels in St. Francois Lagoon out to our anchored mother ship, the *Tam Tam*, for lunch.

It had been quite a morning, this first one of our trip. An hour or so earlier, moved by curiosity and astonishment, I had cast a bonefish fly at the head of some ridiculously long shape cruising the edge of a flat and it turned out to be a seventy- to eighty-pound barracuda which gobbled the fly, screamed around behind my legs, and jumped between Tom and me, no more than twenty feet away, its murderous mouth agape and flailing. Then the thing had run for open water, taking all but four or five wraps of three hundred yards of line and backing with it by the time Donald could bring the skiff up to follow it. I had fought the cuda for fifteen minutes—with growing anxiety about what we would do if I won—before one of the myriad little knives in its mouth cut my leader.

And before the barracuda, I had enjoyed nothing less than the best morning of bonefishing of my life (a rather long life too, it must be said, so much of which has been given over to chasing bonefish that my wife, among others, has argued for years that I need a twelve-step program). Early in the morning the bones had been stacked up along the edges of the flat, waiting for enough water to bring them onto it to feed. The fish reminded me of milling diners lined up outside of Galatoire's in New Orleans, and we caught them as readily as if we had been standing inside that noble restaurant tossing out onto the sidewalk little *pompanos en papillote* on hooks, and then continued to catch them all morning long as they filed in *au table*.

"Great morning," I said to Donald as we tied up to the mother ship. "Unbelievable, really."

"Actually it was a little slow," he said. "But maybe it will pick up this afternoon."

The fanatic French fisherman, Claude, was already on board the *Tam Tam* and bolting his lunch in order to get back out to the flats as quickly as possible. "In the surf near the wreck," he said when I asked him where he had fished. He kept pushing food into his mouth as we talked, and his eyes widened with Gallic emphasis. "Many, *many* beeg bonefeesh. Whaaa! *Huge* bonefeesh. You come back with me now!" He grabbed his fly rods with one hand and a piece of cake with the other.

"After lunch," I told him, looking at the lavish spread of mussel pasta, cold chicken, smoked sailfish, and other goodies that Martin Lewis had laid out in the *Tam Tam*'s cabin. Off our stern, Donald and the other two guides, Jude Morel and Paul Bamboche, were throwing cold cuts and pieces of bread and fruit to a boiling herd of giant trevallies, each of them between twenty and thirty pounds large, and watching that for a few moments had made me ravenous. I started heaping up a plate. Martin handed me a beer.

"Do you ever try to catch those trevallies?" I asked him.

"Lots of people have tried. The buggers are too smart to take a fly."

Aha! I thought, settling back into a divan with my lunch and my beer, so *that's* the nasty in the bran tub, as the English say—the overlooked lugworm in the bait box of fortune (as they also say, who knows why?): mooching, non-fly-eating trevallies just off the stern! There had to be something less than perfect about this Seychelles deal.

An easy-pickings plenitude has always been a major selling point for the Seychelles Islands. After provisioning his boat with three hundred giant tortoises and six hundred coconuts in only four days of 1742, a French captain named Lazare Picault christened Mahe, the largest island of the 115-island archipelago, L'Île d'Abondance (Isle of Abundance). And in an early Brit confrontation with the nasty in the bran tub, John Jourdain, a member of the English

East India Company voyage that first charted the islands, recorded in his journal in 1609 that their crew brought on board "so many tortells as they could carrie. The tortells were good meate, as good as fresh beefe, but after twoe or three meals our men would not eate them because they did looke so uglie before they were boyled."

Scattered over 1,340,000 square kilometers of the Indian Ocean, a thousand miles east of the Kenyan coast and four degrees south of the equator, the Seychelles archipelago was probably discovered by Arabs in the ninth century or before, though the discovery is usually credited to Vasco da Gama in 1502. In the eighteenth century the islands, like so much of the world's real estate, went back and forth between the English and the French until the 1814 Treaty of Paris confirmed British sovereignty over them. In 1903 they became a crown colony. On June 29, 1976, they gained full independence from Great Britain and have prospered since then as a democratic republic.

One of the planet's most beautiful places—a heartbreakingly ravishing combination of rain forests, mountains, beaches, and lagoons—the Seychelles are also one of the remotest and most pristine. Eighty-five of the 115 islands are uninhabited, and 90 percent of the seventy thousand Seychellois (a piquant Creole mixture of African, Asian, and European descent) live on the main island of Mahe. Moreover, 46 percent of the total area of the archipelago has been designated as nature reserve or parkland, indicating the Seychelles government's laudable determination to preserve the islands' traditional purity and abundance.

Specifically, it was the abundance of big game fish that drew Martin Lewis, an early-retired British civil servant, and his wife, Anna, to the Seychelles in 1988. Martin hand built the *Tam Tam* from materials he had shipped over from England, and started selling day charters for sailfish, marlin, and yellowfin tuna out of

Mahe. A sturdy forty-foot by twenty-foot, twin-diesel-powered, fiberglass cruising cat, the boat was built to have a range of a thousand miles-plus, so when the fishing around Mahe started to get crowded, Martin lengthened his charters to long weekends, then weeks, and went further afield in the archipelago after good fishing. But there was scarcely enough market for that fishing to pay the bills. It was a big day when Anna could afford a second pair of flip-flops, and more than once Martin had to beg for throw-away food at the service doors of Mahe restaurants. He was closing in on sixty. He was where he wanted to be, but it seemed impossible to make a living there. The bran-tub nasty had him by the throat.

Then in January of 1988 he took a group of South Africans on a two-month-long exploratory charter some 250 miles southwest of Mahe to a cluster of three islands at the southern tip of the Amirantes chain of the archipelago. Anchored up at night in the lovely seven-mile by four-mile lagoon of one of the three islands, an uninhabited one called St. Francois, Martin and his South Africans started noticing huge schools of bonefish prowling the hard, white sand flats of the lagoon. They waded out and caught a few of those fish on fly rods and realized that they could literally catch as many as they wanted. Martin is no dummy; he knew what people would pay for good bonefishing. In what could only be called a eureka moment, he saw his future—and in it the service doors of restaurants had all become front doors.

Back home, the South Africans talked to French and American friends about what they had found, and within six weeks Martin was deluged with requests for bonefish trips to St. Francois. He took four anglers at a time for Saturday to Saturday live-aboard charters on the *Tam Tam* and found himself working eighteen hours a day, seven days a week. It was not long, of course, before others started to horn in on the business, and out of a legitimate concern for the ecology of the fishery as well as, perhaps, a bit of self-interest, Martin persuaded the Seychelles government to declare the lagoon a sort of national marine park in which only twelve rods at a time would be allowed to fish and all bonefish caught had to be released. To further help his situation, a luxury resort hotel opened in January of 2000 on nearby Alphonse Island, providing his anglers with deluxe digs and Martin with relief from the long hours and constant headaches of live-aboard fishing.

During our week at Alphonse Island Resort, my wife, Patricia, and I were made extremely comfortable in one of the hotel's twenty-five lagoon-side bungalows. We wined and dined elegantly, and swam in the pool. We took walks over deserted beaches and into the lush, steamy interior of the little island to visit an old copra plantation. We bird-watched and biked, played billiards after dinner, and browsed the French coffee-table books laid out in the open air lobby. I also kayaked, made a spectacular wall dive amid turtles, Napoleon fish, and morays, and caught sailfish, yellowfin tuna, and wahoo on board the hotel's big game boat. All of the above made for a splendid week, but not necessarily one for which I would fly some twenty-two hours across ten time zones from my home in Alabama. Nowadays, I do that only in chase of sporting superlatives.

I had heard about the bonefishing at St. Francois from two of the most widely traveled anglers alive, both of whom were left groping for adjectives to describe how superb it was, and yet I went with some misgivings. I believe it was my old friend Kurt Vonnegut who wrote that "Travel is God's dancing lesson." Too often I arrive at some piscatorial ballroom, dancing shoes on, to find that both the band and the instructor have caught the flu that week and gone home. But happily, that was not the case at St. Francois, where the bonefishing truly did turn out to be—in a world of growing parity, as they say in the NFL—what vintage

Patek Philippe is to wristwatches, Hinckley is to sailboats, and Silvano Lattanzi is to men's shoes: a rare and shining ne plus ultra. It was that all week. On our last day it turned into something altogether otherworldly.

We woke to a dropped wind and good sun, and at six thirty Tom and I walked over to the open air dining room where the hotel's magnificent headwaiter, Singh, brought us posh fruit plates and double espressos. The Russian with the young family was breakfasting by himself (call him Ivan). Another Russian (Yuri) had left the resort the day before, a day earlier than scheduled. It was Patricia who noticed that during their time there together Ivan and Yuri never spoke to, or even acknowledged, each other. Both, she learned somehow, had themselves registered as "economists," which Tom claimed with authority was shorthand for Russian Mafia. It just took elemental logic then to piece together the story: Yuri, the hit man, is sent over to terminate Ivan but can't bring himself to do it because of Ivan's adorable three-year-old daughter, and so leaves early to exile himself for the rest of his life in Toledo, Ohio.

Tom and I smiled our relief and best wishes to Ivan on our way out of the dining room, then we bicycled down to the dock to meet the *Tam Tam*, counting our blessings that we were just simple-minded anglers and not Russian "economists."

The steam over to St. Francois, past tiny, perfect Bijoutier, the third island in the Alphonse group, takes around thirty minutes—just enough time to tie on new leaders, transfer more bonefish flies into your wading fanny pack to replace the ones you lost the day before to coral heads or less-than-perfect knots, and to listen to the bonefish-maddened Frenchman describe with much body language three or maybe four of the fish he caught yesterday. When the *Tam Tam* was anchored in the lagoon, Tom and I loaded the gear onto one of the eighteen-foot SeaArk skiffs, and

Jude and Paul, our guides for the day, threaded us through connecting channels to one of the eight or ten flats, most of them
enormous, that lie all around St. Francois.

It was eight thirty when we stepped out of the skiff into ankle-
high water, an hour and a half after dead-low tide. Tom and Paul
elected to stay along the edge of the channel until the rising tide
brought fish onto the flat. Jude and I started off walking east
across the flat to the open water surf about a mile away where
bonefish, many of them whoppers, pile up on an early rising tide.
The morning was fresh, flawless, and crowded with frigate birds
and terns, boobies and gulls, and a few motionless heron fishing
the flat, which itself was thick with life: milkfish, boxfish, rays,
sharks, barracuda, mullet, crabs, sea cucumbers . . . a school of
bonefish? The tide seemed too low for them to be that far up on
the flat, and, to me anyway, the acre or two of flashing tails and
dorsal fins we were looking at seemed way too large a congregation to be bonefish. But as we got closer we saw that it was indeed
a school of bones, a *university* of bones, thrashing, feeding pig-
gishly, and wriggling forward up the flat toward us in water not yet
deep enough to cover their backs, their tails and fins glinting in
the sun like a moving carpet of dimes. Jude and I just stood there
and stared as they approached, and I, for one, was happy that
bonefish don't have teeth.

I had read years ago that legendary angler/chef A. J. McClane
had figured out a method for catching the bottom-feeding bonefish on dry flies—a feat that, for no very good reason, I yearned to
replicate. This seemed the perfect opportunity, with thousands of
bones in front of me in such shallow water that they could not help
but see a fly on the surface.

"Watch this," I said confidently to Jude, who was watching me
with some amusement as I tied on a big Irresistible. "You are
about to learn something new and valuable, my friend." I then

proceeded, of course, to catch bone after bone on mayflies and caddis patterns, a grasshopper, an ant, a marshmallow . . .

Not really. I never even got a look in fifty casts. Jude lost interest in the experiment quickly and began catching bonefish right and left on a carpet-crab fly I had given him; so, concluding finally that A. J. had either been a fibber or knew something I would never know, I tied one on too. After a while, Tom and Paul waded up. The bonefish were still feeding and thrashing out in front of us in water less than a foot deep and, while Tom photographed, Jude and Paul and I slayed them for about an hour and a half—hooking a fish on almost every cast without moving more than thirty yards until the tide came up high enough to disperse the school. The fish we caught averaged an honest five to six pounds, and more than a few were close to ten. It was simply a bonefishing wet dream. It was also a tidy little metaphor for a happy life: The fish were there better than you could possibly hope for; then the tide came up quickly and they were gone.

Some clouds came in and covered the sun on our walk back toward the skiff, but it didn't matter. We came to a place on the flat where bones were streaming in, school after school along the same route, and again we stood more or less in one spot—spotting them at only twenty to thirty feet away when they appeared suddenly but whole, as if willed up like a memory, in keeping with the chimerical nature of the little rascals—and we hooked them on almost every cast for another hour and a half.

I can't tell you how many bonefish I released that morning because after beginning a count with my first I soon abandoned it for seeming gauche and trivial—a serious impoliteness to the experience, the real heart of which was the conscious realization, reoccurring throughout the morning along with both exhilaration and a bit of tristesse, that I was having at that very moment not only the best I had ever had but the best I will ever have of something I passionately love to do. It seemed sort of dumb to try to quantify that.

Neither did I count any of the more technical and difficult fish I caught that afternoon on the outgoing tide, some of them the biggest of the week. Counting only one fish that last day on St. Francois, and that one not a bonefish, was all it took to clinch it as one of the two or three best and most satisfying fishing days of my life.

Watching Jude and Paul throw fruit and bread and chicken bones to the ravening giant trevally after lunch, I had a sudden, brilliant, nasty-in-the-bran-tub-defeating inspiration. I tied a chunky, bright-red tarpon streamer onto a ten-weight outfit, cut off the feathers behind the hook, and timed it so that my fly hit the water just as Jude threw in a handful of watermelon. The rest, as they say, is history.

3

ON THE BITCH GODDESS HIGHWAY THROUGH THE LAND OF GIANTS AND BACANS

"*Haciendo fiaca!*" exclaimed Jorge Alejandro Graziosi. "It means enjoying life without problems the way we are now—doing things in a relaxed way, without stress. We believe that is the way to live all the time; to live like a *bacan!*"

He finished his wine and passed the glass over his shoulder to Bryce to refill in the backseat. Jorge put both hands for a change on the steering wheel of the Brazilian Suburban and skidded through a sequence of turns on the fierce gravel road as if he were skiing the truck through a giant slalom course. The speedometer, which I had grown accustomed to staring at, did not drop below 140 kilometers per hour. Then Jorge took the filled wine glass back from Bryce, ate a few pieces of cheese and sausage off the china plate in his lap, and pushed the rig back up to 160 k.p.h.

"And what is a *bacan?*" I asked him, taking another glass of wine from Bryce myself in an effort to enjoy our high-velocity lunch in a relaxed way, without stress.

"Someone who lives very well without working too hard at it. You work, but on your own terms, and with much time given to pleasures other than work—skiing, polo, fly fishing, good wines, cigars. A *bacan* is a bon vivant with or without money."

"Like Bebe Anchorena and Jorge Donovan?" I said, naming a couple of legendary Argentine high-livers who fit the definition as well as Jorge Alejandro himself did.

"Exactly!"

After we finished the cheese and sausage, Bryce served our plates with slices of roasted chicken, a salad of rice and peas, and thick chunks of rare *lomo*, the unspeakably delicious Argentine sirloin. At volume, B. B. King was singing "Playing with My Friends." Outside the car, the increasingly empty Patagonian steppes sped by; inside, the plates and wine glasses whisked back and forth across the front seat—the piquant sauce, napkins, more *lomo*, more chicken.

"Our chicken in the U.S. doesn't taste like this anymore," commented Tom Montgomery, who was sharing the backseat with Bryce, a young American trout guide who worked for Jorge. Tom was gripping his plate so that his knuckles showed white. "We shoot it up with too many drugs."

"Here it is *illegal* to shoot up chickens," said Jorge Alejandro indignantly.

"And what is the law here governing speed limits?" I asked him.

He looked across the seat at me, grinning like a *bacan* wolf. "On *La Cuarenta* there is no law, and no one to enforce it either. You drive as fast as you can without rolling the vehicle. It is safer on *La Cuarenta* to drive fast."

That was *one* thing about the road the guide books had not mentioned. *La Cuarenta* (The Forty) is the fear-and-trembling nickname used throughout Argentina for Route 40. The longest highway in Argentina and one of the longest in South America, The Forty stretches from near Argentina's border with Bolivia in the north to Rio Gallegos, the southernmost town on the country's mainland. Running for its entire length just east, and often within view, of the Cordillera of the Andes, The Forty is one of South America's most scenic highways, and also one of its most hazardous. Only one third of the road's forty-five-hundred-plus kilometers are paved; the rest are covered in car-eating gravel. Beware of rain on these gravel sections, say the guidebooks; beware of sliding out on turns and rolling your vehicle; beware of total absence of guardrails, of broken windshields, blown tires, punctured fuel tanks; carry a generous reserve of fuel, at least two spare tires, an air pump, sealing paste or quince jelly for the fuel tank, oil, brake fluid, food. And while on the long, *long* stretch of gravel Route 40 running through southern Patagonia, these books stress, you can add to your worries an all but immaculate absence of villages, tow trucks, service stations, and other vehicles: "In case of need," says one book, "the traveler will find little if any help."

There are people who are attracted to such roads for their own sake. I am not among them. But ever since I started traveling in Argentina some twenty-five years ago, I have heard my Argentine friends Maita Barranechea and Buby Calvo speak with passion about the "real Patagonia" south of Esquel, the deserted plateaus and endless, wind-scoured plains running all the way to the bottom of the continent and comprising one of the largest scarcely populated places on earth. Finally, I just had to see it—even if it meant two weeks of driving on *La Cuarenta*.

"It is a road with a soul," Buby had written in an e-mail. "We will learn the soul of *La Cuarenta!*"

"I hope you don't learn it as well as the two hitchhikers I talked to a couple of years ago south of here," said Jorge. "They had been waiting three days for a vehicle going south. Unfortunately, I was going north."

There were a few tan hills to the west shaped like a senorita's backside, and beyond them occasionally you could see the ragged silhouette of the Andes. To the east and south, where we were going, the high desert plateau stretched out flat and limitless as the sea—an occasional cow or sheep grazing, a small herd of the wild llamas called guanaco, no vegetation higher than homely, yellow, sage-brush-like clumps of weed the size of coral heads. It was, perhaps, a countryside of shy beauty, I decided—an acquired taste after the verdant, jewel-like valley north of Esquel where we had spent the past two days trout fishing and living like *bacans* out of Jorge Alejandro's splendid fishing lodge, Arroyo Claro.

There we had eaten bankside lunches of veal Milanese and lamb, and brilliant midnight dinners prepared by Jorge's wildly inventive young chef, Ariel. We had floated the preternaturally clear Rio Azul that holds brook trout, rainbows, and browns up to nine pounds, and landlocked salmon up to fifteen, and caught one eighteen- to twenty-inch rainbow after another—strong, chrome-bright, rose-striped, tail-walking fish—with the air full of condors, southern lapwings, ibis, and ashy-headed geese. And we had caught chunky, yellow-bellied browns the next day on the five-mile-long Rivadavia River, a twisting, turquoise beauty running between two lakes through dense beech forests in Los Alerces National Park, and cut the meat of that day as close to the bone as we did the joint of rare lamb for lunch.

We had seen Jorge's ranch in Cholila—Butch Cassidy's and the Sundance Kid's old hideout—and met his thirty-eight-year-old wife who was pregnant with his fourth child. After a decade of his luck running muddy, life for this dean of South American trout guides was again as robust as a good Argentine Malbec, and we had found him enjoying it again in the proud, feline, sybaritic style that seems locked like a gene into so many Argentine men. He was as curly-haired, strong, and witty as ever, and his very calm blue eyes did not even look dented by the past ten years. A sticker on his truck read, in English, "Getting Old is Not for Sissies." When I asked him how old he was, Jorge Alejandro said: "The men say I am fifty-five; the women say twenty-five."

At the town of Alto Rio Senguer we turned west off The Forty onto Highway 57 leading to Lago La Plata near the Chilean border. We ate brownies for dessert, drank more wine, and listened to B. B. King's *Blues Summit* tape again. After a while we were into the foothills. The road began to wind, but Jorge kept the Suburban between 140 and 160 k.p.h. The sky was slate colored with streaks of blue and there was snow on the tops of some of the hills. Traffic had gone from a vehicle every half hour or so to nothing at all, and the day seemed as replete with time as the road did with emptiness. It occurred to me that stress and driving slowly were the same way of worrying down here, and that the vast countryside and slow time would have to break you of both.

When we finally arrived at Lago La Plata, we had driven 350 miles in about half the time it would have taken me to do it. We drank *café con leche* with the owner of some tourist cabins, then Jorge and Bryce left to drive back home to Arroyo Claro. They had food and wine and blues tapes enough for the return trip, and there was still all the time you could want from the day.

"Living the moment is the thing in Argentina, particularly down here along The Forty," said Magdalena Bustillo. She was sitting on a piece of driftwood on the shore of Lago La Plata, wearing chest waders, a beret, and a fishing vest. She was tall and slim and black haired. She smoked a cigarette and pulled her long thighs to her chest. Her voice was husky and deep. Her eyes had clearly seen a lot, and there was a fine, kind-looking forbearance in them. "In

America you have your future in a box. Here we spend the future. We don't even own a box."

Magdalena was the manager, and a part-time fishing guide at Bahia Arenal, a $6 million wilderness lodge carved out of beech forest at the western end of the immense blue Andean lake where Jorge had dropped us off. In its utter remoteness, even by *La Cuarenta*'s standards, Bahia Arenal is a place you really have to want to get to; but once there, it is easy to imagine taking up residence for a while.

The lodge is the last big statement on life and how energetically it ought to be lived by an elfin eighty-seven-year-old business tycoon named Eduardo Mayer. After starting Argentina's first and most important insurance company, after opening a major bank and bringing MasterCard into the country, after beginning aviation and doll-manufacturing companies and seeing the world, sailing the Mediterranean for a month each year and owning twenty planes, Mayer decided to do one final, monumental thing that everyone told him could not be done: create a world-class luxury lodge in the most remote and pristine place he could find in southern Patagonia. It took four years to locate the right property, and five years to build the lodge, in an almost unimaginably ambitious act of seizing and occupying. "It was *fantastico*," is how Mayer describes the project. "God gives a lot, but he doesn't give everything. What he doesn't give that you want, you must take."

Bahia Arenal sits on five thousand acres fronting the lake, surrounded on three sides by peaks of the Chilean Andes. To get to it you drive forever on Route 40, and then are transported seventeen kilometers down the lake on Mayer's yacht. The lodge has six large bedrooms and baths overlooking the lake and a forty-eight-hundred-square-foot main building. It has a three-star chef, towel-warming racks, showerheads the size of dinner plates, Jacuzzi tubs, and someone pouring you more champagne every time you turn around. It has a large, young, happy, and accommodating staff managed by Magdalena, and it offers trail riding, nature hikes, water sports, and fishing in the lake. But what Bahia Arenal mostly offers is profound privacy, and that is exactly what Eduardo Mayer had in mind. "Everywhere," he says, "what the rich now want most is a place to get away. Privacy is the great luxury of the twenty-first century."

The lodge had been open for only four months. Magdalena was not certain if it could be commercially viable or not, given its gigantic overhead, but she liked Mayer and trusted his vision. "He sees things before other people do and then he works very, very hard at them. Mayer loves *things*, not the money. He is a *bacan* but *work* is living well for him. Work is his passion, his creativity."

Nor was she certain how long she would stay locked away here. Her dream was to build a little house in Junin, north of *La Cua-renta*. A cabin. "Build it myself, and fish the Chimehuin. Have a garden. I can grow strawberries and raspberries, produce something and sell it. Work with guiding fishermen in the summer."

She had started fly fishing in 1990 when she married an American trout guide. They spent half the year guiding, fishing, and traveling in Montana, and the other half doing the same thing in Patagonia. Then, a few months ago, she and her American were divorced, but she still had the fly fishing. She was passionate about that, and therefore happy to be where she was for the time being, with or without a husband. Lago La Plata contained what is said to be the largest single-lake population of brook trout in the world, and Magdalena, and Pablo and Jeremy, the two young guides who worked under her, had it practically all to themselves and their clients at Bahia Arenal.

While Tom and I were there we wade-fished coves and points and stream mouths in the lake, and caught lots of dark, ornately colored brookies, whose ancestors originally came to Argentina from Sebago Lake in Maine. They were very strong-fighting fish of a pound or two, and we caught them on crane fly imitations where the cold, green shoreline water dropped off to depth, and killed a few to eat for breakfast and for shore lunches with sausages and cheese and wine cooled in the lake.

"Wherever I go, I'll be fine," said Magdalena, staring out at the vast Lago La Plata. "I don't need to be married again." She lit another cigarette and shrugged. "My kind of life is not good for marriage."

When we had finished talking, she waded into the lake and began to fish, casting a fine, tight loop of line, pushing out the fly into a rising wind.

Joined by my wife, Patricia, Buby and Maita, and Janet and Ben Mixon from South Carolina, we left Lago La Plata driving a diesel Toyota pickup and a Jeep Cherokee and continued south on *La Cuarenta*. I drove the Jeep, and tried hard to keep in view at least the dust of the Toyota, which Buby was handling, à la Jorge, with fervency and skill. For the first few hours, driving at 100 k.p.h. on the loose, ungraded gravel felt to me rather like skating on corrugated ice at night in a pair of borrowed skates. I was reminded frequently by Patricia that a higher percentage of motorists were killed, mostly in rollovers, on this road than on any in Argentina despite the absence of traffic, and that the rental car company had refused to insure us against rolling the vehicle and would charge us an automatic $4,000 if we did so, assuming we were still alive. Reminded of those things, it seemed crazy to try to keep up with Buby—who, like Jorge and maybe every Argentine male over sixteen, had driven race cars at one time in his life—but I couldn't help myself. *La Cuarenta* herself seemed to demand it. And after a while my grip on the wheel grew lighter; I began flying over cattle guards, accelerating through the turns, braking only on straightaways, and turning into the skids as Jorge had coached Montgomery and me to do.

After a couple of hours of dead-heading through a vast bowl, flat and featureless as a pie plate, the road rose and snaked, calling itself on proud yellow signs a *"Camino Sinuoso,"* onto a high desert plateau with a rim around it of flat-topped *mesetas*. There were lots of rhea there, the Argentine ostrich, and hare and small herds of the long-necked guanaco who give you long feminine stares of offended hauteur as you speed by—all of them working full-time jobs finding what they could to eat on a poor land made ever poorer from decades of overgrazing sheep, and, more recently, by drought.

At the bar in the Hotel Almacen—the only building of any kind between Lago La Plata and the town of Rio Mayo—a gaucho named Juan Carlos told us that it had not rained there for five or six years, and the last time it snowed was over a decade ago. Juan Carlos was a squat, resigned man with a wide, muscular upper body and stubby legs. In better days he had been employed by one of the local estancias. Now all but one of those estancias had been abandoned, and Juan Carlos ranched three hundred sheep of his own and waited for his savings to run out. It was not only the drought that was killing southern Patagonia, he said, but the government, most of whose representatives should be rounded up and shot. "I myself should be president of Argentina," said Juan Carlos. "If I were in charge, everything would be working correctly in sixty days." He grinned, showing us a mouthful of unattended teeth.

"Juan Carlos for president!" said Maita.

"Okay," said Juan Carlos and grinned again.

Outside the wind flayed the flat, stingy land and howled around the chipped and rounded stucco corners of the Hotel Almacen. Juan Carlos left the hotel with us.

What would he do, I asked him, when his savings ran out?

"We are tough," he said. "Argentines are survivors." His horse was tied to a fence in front of the hotel, and a sheep dog, lying curled in the dust beside the horse, sprang up and began to bark. Juan Carlos struggled to get his short leg high enough to put a foot in the stirrup, then he swung up into a bright-white sheepskin saddle. He pulled the horse's head around and waved his *rebenque*, the gaucho's quirt, at us. "No matter how poor we are here though, we always have food. If there were three hundred of you, I could feed you a sheep apiece."

He cracked his horse on the flank with the *rebenque* and trotted off, the sheep dog running out ahead.

In this part of Patagonia the gauchos mount the carcasses of dogs that kill sheep onto fences. They make their dogs watch the impaling of the live offender onto the fence post, its slow death and slower decomposition, believing those other dogs might take the lesson to heart. That, said Buby, is the kind of president Juan Carlos would be. "Who knows? Maybe it would work."

We drove through Rio Mayo, the once thriving sheep-shearing capital of Argentina, now a ruined, dispirited place, and then up a long stretch of *camino sinuoso* to a high desert that would have looked like southern Arizona but for the ostriches and guanaco, where driving began to feel like a form of penance—a high-speed hair shirt—and continued to feel that way through the town of Perito Moreno. I went to sleep that night in a little guest house called Estancia Telken—where a fall of volcanic ash that still covered much of the landscape had killed seven thousand of the owner's eleven thousand sheep a few years before—wondering if maybe Job had grown up in this neck of the woods.

If the stretch of Route 40 we had already traveled was the most forlorn and desolate stretch of road any of us had ever seen, it was not even a close second to the five-hundred-kilometer section between Estancia Telken and the little town of Tres Lagos. *La Cuarenta* went, so to speak, from a thin and flinty but vaguely attractive older woman to a cackling, desiccated hag within the blink of an eye: What shoulders there had been disappeared; the gravel was even looser and crazier; the road seemed as baked and forgotten as a piece of month-old roadkill on the vast and empty steppes where nothing grew but a few tangled clumps of weed.

Other than a few little puckered rock holes in both windshields, the old witch had left us pretty much unbothered though, until the Siberian Plateau, an area south of the town of Baja Caracoles, where it came into my head, oddly, that you could make fifty John Ford Westerns at the same time here, Indians, stagecoaches, and all, and none of them would ever know the others were shooting.

Buby and Maita were in the Cherokee with Patricia and me. We had last seen Tom and the Mixons in the Toyota about two hours before when we gassed up the vehicles in Baja Caracoles, and we believed they were only a few minutes behind us when we pulled off the road into the desert for a picnic lunch. We waited for a half hour, then a half hour more; then we sat in a small depression in the land, using the Cherokee as a windbreak, and had our lunch. While we were eating, Buby flagged down a car that miraculously happened by, going south, and the driver said he had passed no vehicles standing or moving since Baja Caracoles, leading us to conclude that Tom and the Mixons had somehow taken a wrong turn and were now headed either back north or east toward the Atlantic coast. In this landscape as devoid of features as the open ocean, we realized, they might drive for hours without recognizing their mistake.

When an hour and a half had passed we decided to wait for one more half hour, and I went for a walk. While eating lunch, Maita had pointed out some chips of obsidian lying around the sand, some of which appeared to be worked. Though it seemed about as likely as stumbling onto Tom and the Mixons, I wanted to find an arrowhead, so I zigzagged into the desert with my head down.

The sixteenth-century inhabitants of southern Patagonia, the Tehuelche Indians, were giants, according to Antonio Pigafetta, who was the first of a long line of Europeans to write about the place with starry-eyed wonder. As the chronicler of Magellan's 1520 voyage to the New World, Pigafetta described the men Magellan's crew encountered on the island of Tierra del Fuego as being eleven feet tall, running faster than horses, eating raw flesh, including "rats without first skinning them," and drinking half buckets of water at once. The word Patagonia is said to have originated with Magellan exclaiming, "Ha! Patagon (Big Foot)!" to the first of these natives he met. For the next couple of hundred years, southern Patagonia, a "country of black fogs and whirlwinds at the end of the habited world," was known as the Land of Giants to spellbound Europeans who learned about it through chronicles of the voyages of Drake, Cavendish and Davis, Sarmiento de Gamboa, Sebald de Weert, and others in much the same skewed way that some of us now learn about real life through soap operas.

If indeed the Tehuelches were once giants, they had shrunk by 1823 when Charles Darwin traveled through southern Patagonia and described them as being not only normal in stature but so barbaric, so wrenched, that "one can hardly ask oneself to believe they are fellow creatures." Only seventy years later a version of that sentiment from the developer of *Origin of Species* helped to contribute to the total extirpation of the Indians there. To those Indians, the sheep introduced into their land by the Europeans around the turn of the century looked enough like guanaco to hunt and eat, and after a while they grew partial to roasted lamb. The ranchers' response to this was to offer one pound sterling for every dead-Indian ear. Armed with Winchesters and the slogan "The survival of the fittest," men such as Alexander (the Red Pig) MacLennan had little trouble bagging as many as fourteen ears a day. Those natives that the ranchers and mercenaries didn't kill were herded into missions where they died more slowly from tuberculosis, smallpox, and other diseases, and by 1920 there were almost no Indians of any size left in the Land of the Giants.

The desert I wandered into, looking at the ground, was littered with bones and occasional shards of obsidian glinting in the sand. The obsidian flakes had been left there by forbears of the giants, the nomadic bands of Indians who first traveled these steppes between ten thousand and a thousand years ago. The day before, we had visited the Cave of the Hands, the most important prehistoric art site in Argentina, where hundreds of Tehuelche hands, outlined on rock walls in red and white pigments, waved hello, or good-bye, from thousands of years ago. Now I was looking at pieces of stone flaked off, perhaps, by some of those hands.

The writer Paul Theroux commented on the mind-bending shift of perspective you have on the Patagonian plains between looking down at the ground, where everything is very small, and then looking up at the enormous landscape. And W. H. Hudson, the ornithologist and author of *Idle Days in Patagonia*, wrote that if you look *for* anything at all in that landscape, you are missing the point: that the peculiar magic of the Patagonian steppes is to swallow the looker and transport him into an animistic suspension of intellect and self, perhaps the same as the Peace of God, which is the best possible anodyne to life everywhere else.

Just as I was about to turn around and walk back to the Cherokee, with the wind keening around me like dispossessed spirits, I looked one last time from the large to the bone-cluttered small,

and there poking out of the sand was a perfect Tehuelche arrow-head.

Tom Montgomery and the Mixons finally caught up with us about a hundred kilometers down the road, where we had stopped at the only building between Baja Caracoles and Tres Lagos—a whitewashed, weather-beaten stone hotel, bar, restaurant, and service station called La Horqueatas. Ben Mixon explained that they had had a flat tire, and rather than take a chance continuing with no spare, they had driven back to Baja Caracoles to have it fixed.

La Horqueatas turned out to be a providential place for our friends to show up safe and sound. It belonged to a tall, saturnine man, long jawed and gaunt with deep-set blue eyes, named Alberto and known locally as the "Saint of Route 40." Alberto had grown up nearby. As a truck driver of cattle and sheep, he kept passing this old building—which had boomed as a hotel in the 1920s, '30s, and '40s but been deserted for years—and always felt a pang of sorrow that it was no longer open for travelers. So two and a half years ago he bought and restored it. Now he and his wife, Sandra, kept the place open twenty-four hours a day every day of the year as a gathering place for locals, but more important as an aid station for motorists along *La Cuarenta*. Alberto had the only phone within 350 kilometers. "Our duty," he said, "is never to be closed, to be always available for help." So far this season he had helped out over a dozen drivers of rolled and broken-down vehicles.

Alberto stood behind his bar drinking from a water glass full of wine and smoking Marlboros. Sandra stood very close beside him and one of their three children sat on the bar playing with an ashtray. Alberto showed us a recent newspaper article that called him "a friend in the middle of nowhere." My Spanish not being up to it, I asked Maita to ask him what he got out of being that. He told her, "I love it. I love being there to help people." A gaucho at the end of the bar laughed and said that Alberto was too good to be true, a man with an *"immenso corazon"*—a huge heart.

Alberto charged ten dollars a night for a room for two people, five dollars for a *tortilla de papa*, a potato-and-onion omelet big enough to feed three people, and half a peso for a glass of *cana quemada*, the strong, sweet liquor of the gauchos. I asked him what he thought of the haggard, half-mad old road outside, and what it was like to live in such a place. "Nothing is difficult for us," he said, smiling for the first time. "We have fellowship and family and love. And the road, it is *beautiful*. Every season, year-round, it is beautiful. Also it is fun living on *La Cuarenta*. My wife and children and friends and I are never bored."

The Saint of Route 40 walked outside with us when we left and showed us his "vehicle of mercy." It was a very old blue dump truck with a taped windshield, no headlights, and a tied-down hood.

Casimiro Ferrari had spent 182 nights of his fifty-nine years in a sleeping bag on Andean peaks. In 1974 he led the Italian team that first climbed Cerro Torre, arguably the most difficult climb in the Andes, and that first ascent embroiled him in years of controversy about which he will only say, "Mountains are pure, but mountain climbers are not."

Casimiro grew up climbing near his birthplace of Lake Como, Italy. Since then he has climbed all over Europe and in the Himalayas, but the Argentine Andes are his favorite mountains. "Virgin daughters," he calls them, with his talent for speaking in metaphorical aphorisms. "The Himalayas are grandes dames." He began climbing the virgin daughters thirty-five years ago. Five years ago, he moved to Argentina and bought a sixty-thousand-acre estancia called Punta del Lago just off Route 40 between Tres Lagos and El Calafate, overlooking Lake Viedma. The estancia, which he had recently and indifferently opened to paying guests, is eighty kilometers from Chalten, the Chamonix of Argentina, and around a hundred kilometers from both Cerro Torre and Fitz Roy, the lovely, arrowhead-shaped peaks on the logo of Patagonia clothing.

There were fifteen hundred sheep on Punta del Lago, as well as cattle and horses, but Casimiro had income from a wire factory he owned in Italy and did not need to make a profit from ranching. For this he was grateful, because the puma in this area of Patagonia—preying on sheep from the nearby Glaciers National Park, where they were protected—would finish you off if the wool prices didn't. When he moved here, he said, he needed the work of the ranch; now he was tired of it. But he never tired of the virgin daughters: There were so many new ways to enjoy them now that he no longer cared whether or not he reached their tops.

Casimiro lit a new cigarette off the butt of an old one in his kitchen and said: "Climbing mountains is like love: When you are young, you enjoy it in one way; when you are older, in a different way."

He was presently married to an Argentine woman who spent much of her time at her family's estancia down the road. He prized his solitude, he said, and sometimes went for weeks without seeing anyone. Yet he was spoken of everywhere we went on *La Cuarenta* as one of the most loved men in southern Argentina, and on the night we spent at Punta del Lago, his farmhouse was crowded with people, including two Italian climbing friends of his, burly men with blunt hands and manners and boxer's eyes. Dressed in warm-up suits, they were helping Casimiro cook when we arrived around seven in the evening. Casimiro told us to go put our things in whatever bedrooms might still be available. Patricia and I found a small one in the attic with two little beds, each covered with four or five rough blankets, and a Swiss view of the lake and the snow-tipped mountains behind it. The house was full of climbing trophies, rocks and fossils taken from the mountains, and photographs of wind-blown slopes with ant-like lines of roped humans on them. It had the feel of a small, virile, cheerfully off-hand mountaineering hostel rather than a guest house, and Casimiro was clearly ill-suited to innkeeping.

He was around five feet six inches tall, wiry, hard, and graceful, with a high-mileage, good-humored face. He wore a red down vest and his fly, as with many Argentine men, was unzipped. We talked in the kitchen while he and the two Italian climbers cooked. Casimiro lit one cigarette off the last and talked about the difficulty and physical suffering of the twenty-day-long Cerro Torre first ascent. Then around ten o'clock we went into the dining room, where Casimiro sat at the head of the table and continued to talk. We had a pasta-and-egg soup, bread, and the Italian smoked beef called *bresaola*, then a salad, a pasta, and fried liver and onions. There were a few bottles of sweet white wine on the table and a pitcher of Orangina, which Casimiro mixed with his wine.

The Indians of this land, he said, were exterminated exactly as if they were puma. He himself hated the puma whenever he found some of his sheep murdered by one, but he could not bring himself to kill them. Last week a skunk had killed his hen and eaten her eggs. Casimiro had gone for his rifle, but then changed his mind. He said the question was exactly the same as it had been with the Indians: Who had more right to be here? And it was not a question you could answer easily after a certain age. He believed it was young men who made the decision to exterminate the Tehuelches.

For desert we had chocolate from Italy and pears from Casimiro's tree outside, and then pickled cherries and brandy. I told Casimiro that he lived very well, like a *bacan*. He grinned and said, "In the mountains you learn to value yourself. If you don't value yourself, you live a very short life." He said he could not understand people who were bored with life. There were too many interesting things to do. In Italy, for example, he had raised and trained English setters and had won the first all-European field trial, held in Belgium. Too many things to do, he said again, and our time to do them is always very short. He had stomach cancer, for which he had undergone two operations, he told us, sipping his brandy. Now he had very little stomach left. He made a circle with a forefinger and thumb. And very little time.

La Cuarenta does not end at the town of El Calafate, fewer than two hundred miles from the bottom of the Argentina mainland, but the cackling old shrew becomes socialized again there with pavement and traffic, and continues down the last bit of southern Patagonia to Rio Gallegos hushed and sane, The Forty in name only.

We gassed up and drank excellent *café con leche* from a service station coffee machine in El Calafate, a thriving, likeable town on Lago Argentino. Then we drove west along the south shore of the lake into Los Glaciares National Park. The road ended at a boat launch a few hundred meters across from where the thirty-kilometer-long by five-kilometer-wide Perito Moreno glacier thrust its huge rotting nose into the lake. The day was blue and windless and the lake calm, with charcoal, purple, and silver mountains hovering over it. The crenelated snout of the glacier, rising in jagged creases more than a hundred feet above the lake, went from the white of life at its top to the sky blue of dreams midway down to the cobalt of death where it met the water. It was possible to see it as the place to which all our traveling had brought us, and to dedicate at least three or four days to gazing at it. Instead, we took a boat across to the glacier's southern edge where we met two young guides, Jose Pera and Flavio Renzacci, shouldered fifty-pound packs, and started out on a hike following the glacier's southern moraine to our tent camp for the next two nights.

The six-and-a-half-hour walk, for Patricia, me, and the Mixons, at least, was punishing and hazardous—in the same ways as shockingly, exhilaratingly different from what we thought of as hiking as Route 40 was from what we thought of as a road. The moraine was a rising, pathless jumble of slippery rocks and boulders with steep ups and downs, on some of which it took only one glance downward to know that if you fell there, you died. In a couple of places where the moraine was impassable we strapped on crampons and walked on the glacier, over and around the first seracs and crevasses Patricia and the Mixons had ever seen.

The camp we finally reached at eight o'clock that night was in a beech forest just off the glacier, hard by a mountain stream and picketed by soaring peaks and hanging glaciers. It was used occasionally by Jose and his father, who had arranged our trek, as a base camp for their mountain climbing, and we were only the third commercial group they had brought there in twelve years of operating treks on the glacier. Why not more, I asked Jose, given the splendid beauty and isolation of the place? "Too difficult," said Jose. "Too dangerous."

"Oh," I said.

There was a tarp-covered lean-to with a woodstove, and beside it a fire pit ringed with stones. We set up our tents and sleeping bags under the beeches, then drank wine and ate hard sausages and ravioli around the fire. Patricia and I left the fly to our tent open, and went to sleep listening to the rustle of the stream.

We spent the next day exploring the glacier in crampons— examining and marveling at it in hushed voices as if it were some giant sleeping animal. We picked our way over knobs and rounded hillocks of ice, through bowls, and around steep, crowded spires of seracs. We stepped over crevasses, some of them bottomless, Listerine-blue gashes, and over streams that ran just beneath the surface of the ice and surfaced occasionally into cerulean pools. On this rare second lovely day of mountain weather in a row, the glacier seemed a welcoming, tender, and feminine thing in its round, gleaming curves, its vulvaic creases, and slumberous stretching toward the lake. It could be otherwise, Flavio pointed out—more unwelcoming than one could imagine—and I believed him. He had very red cheeks and his nickname was Manzana, or apple; like Jose, he was preposterously graceful on the ice. During the walk back to camp, he pointed out a little earwig-like insect sunning itself on the lip of a crevasse. It was the only thing that lived on the glacier, Manzana told us: It ate algae, and glycerine in its cells kept it from freezing. The bug put me in mind of Alberto, the Saint of Route 40—at home and happily adapted to all of the seasons and moods of a place where no one else wanted to live.

Luciano Pera gave each of us a big, congratulatory hug when we arrived back down from the glacier at the camp on the southwest shore of the lake from which he conducted his tours. The camp was in a grove of beeches only a hundred meters from a bustling boat dock, but it looked like a remote mountain outpost for a bunch of merry revolutionaries. There was a big photograph of Che Guevara hanging in the bunkhouse, one of three or four log buildings so simple and folded into the setting they seemed to have grown there. There was a homemade icebox and a rubber hose bringing water downhill from a cistern. There were a few chairs and benches made from beech logs, stacks of canned goods, and many rolls of toilet paper. Hanging inside the buildings and lying around outside were chainsaws, cow skulls, crampons, climbing ropes and packs, ice axes, wrenches, files, raincoats, and juggling batons. At the center of all of this was a world of meat cooking on a grill over a big bonfire, and a dwarf playing a guitar and singing.

Also well—and profitably—adapted to the glacier, was Luciano, Jose's father. Like his good friend Casimiro Ferrari, Luciano was born in Italy and started climbing there when he was a child. He came to Argentina for the climbing in 1960, and was Jorge Graziosi's partner in a roped fall that nearly killed them both. Twelve years ago he negotiated an exclusive lease with Glaciers National Park to conduct boat tours of Perito Moreno and to take tourists out onto the ice for hour-and-a-half-long "mini treks." Now his company, Ice and Adventure, handled twelve tours a day of sixteen to twenty people who had to book days and sometimes weeks in advance.

There is no meal in the world as much to my taste as an Argentine *asado*, or barbecue, and after our six-hour walk down the glacier, I fell on this one—equally on the grilled chicken and beef and sweetbreads, the chorizo and blood sausages—like a Patagonian giant. A transparent *bacan*, Luciano watched us with pleasure as we devoured his food and threw back his wine. He was short, powerful, and happy, with silvering hair. When I asked his age, he answered in much the same way as his old friend Jorge Graziosi had two weeks earlier: He jumped out of his chair and did a full squat on one leg, holding the other out in front of him parallel to the ground; then he stood smoothly back up. "As long as I can do that, I am twenty-five," he said.

He told us his business was doing very well and could only do better. A new runway was being finished at the airport at El Calafate that would accommodate jumbo jets. Very soon there would be direct daily flights to and from Buenos Aires that would change things greatly all over southern Patagonia, opening it up to a scale of tourism that was hard to imagine now. *La Cuarenta* would be redundant, or finally paved over, or both. Or she might find a new youth and purpose in tourist traffic—who knew? The road that had helped keep Patagonia Patagonia—its countryside as wild and unpeopled as when the Tehuelches wandered it—might fall away in pieces, like the calving snout of the glacier, into some new life.

The boat that took us across the lake to the parking lot where we had left our dusty, paint-chipped, windshield-cracked vehicles—each now with over two thousand kilometers of Route 40 on its odometer—was crowded with mini-trekkers, but no one seemed to be watching when a giant chuck of Perito Moreno fell off into the gelid, turquoise water. We heard a boom and a tremendous splash. We all looked up, silent as penitents, at the same time to see a mist of spray hanging in the air, waves bearing down as though driven by a forty-knot wind, and then, after a moment, a new iceberg bobbing in the lake.

Everyone cheered.

4

FISHING THE GONE FLORIDA

Tommy and Chris Robinson cut their engines well before the mouth of the main lagoon and we drifted for a few minutes while Montgomery got his cameras ready in Tommy's boat. In Chris's, I tied on a gold spoon fly and stripped out fly line onto the bow deck. The early December morning was calm and so foggy that we had had to search for the entrance to the network of lagoons. Now in the white fog and stillness that erased the seam between water and air we could have been floating on a cloud, or in the pipe smoke of an old nostalgic fishing dream.

The Robinson brothers stood up on the platforms over their engines and began poling Montgomery and me toward the lagoon—where the tide was just right; where they had recently found lots of tailing fish; where the lustrous first promise of a new fishing day waited. The fog thinned before we reached the mouth and the features of the land on either side of it began to emerge: dunes and cabbage palms, dense scrub and live-oak forests on the inland side, virgin stands of pine. In the past two days of splendid Keys-style, shallow-water fly fishing, we had not seen another angler and we knew we would not see one here either—where there were no people, no roads, no boats, no buildings; only water and pristine land, birds and fish—and the lifting fog revealed in all that more dream, not less. I thought: If we find even a single tailing fish to complete this anachronistic perfection I may just send for my wife and bird dogs.

Belize? The Yucatan? Out-island Bahamas? This was Florida— and not a condo, a Jet Ski, or a sunburned tourist in a Disney World T-shirt in sight.

Who of us has never dreamed of fishing the Gone Florida—the Everglades of Dimock, Hemingway's Gulf Stream off Key West, Homosassa before the hordes, the Keys of Joe Brooks—of finding yourself blessedly in front of the curve in some charming, unde-veloped town with a comfortable old wide-porch hotel, a good bar, a fine but inexpensive oyster house, gamefish in the multitudes of yesteryear, and no one else there but you to angle for them? Well, I for one have certainly dreamed of it, which is why Apalachicola felt familiar to me the first time I laid eyes on it.

Located an hour or so west of Tallahassee in the Florida Pan-handle, Apalachicola is an irresistible little town of about four thousand residents in a county of fewer than ten thousand inhabi-tants and not a single stoplight. During the three decades preced-ing the Civil War, the town boomed as a cotton-shipping center and became the third largest port on the Gulf Coast. It has seen booms in sponges, timber, turpentine, and commercial fishing since, but all of them were followed by busts, and by the early 1990s, bypassed west to south by Interstate Highway 10, the area had come to regard itself as "The Forgotten Coast."

Now that coast is being remembered again, by real estate de-velopers among others, and Apalachicola is on the cusp of a new boom, this one occasioned partly by a sports-fishing resource, which in variety and quality is hard to match anywhere else in the

state. In the Apalachicola River are bass and bream. Offshore are billfish, king mackerel, cobia, amberjack, grouper, and snapper. And inshore, on the flats of Apalachicola and St. Joe Bays and in the saltwater creeks, are pompano, jack crevalle, sheepshead, tarpon, speckled trout, and redfish. As a result of emergency redfish-conservation measures initiated in the 1980s and the inshore commercial fishing-net ban passed into Florida law in 1995, the latter two species are there now in numbers and sizes that haven't been seen in years.

At this moment Apalachicola is Key West at some equivalent moment in the 1960s, or Livingston, Montana, in the 1970s, an unspoiled place of real flavor and character where you can live well and have superb fishing practically to yourself—the kind of unpeopled and unconfined richness of angling possibilities that remind you of what your imagination first loved about the sport. It is a dispiriting but defining fact of this world that places do not stay that way for long. But for the time being, the authentic experience of Gone Florida fishing is there to be had in Apalachicola.

To provide that experience the town has everything it needs and no more. It has one just-right hotel in the Gibson Inn, built in 1907 and recently restored, with its lively bar and one of the best porches in Florida for an after-dinner cigar. It has the Boss Oyster restaurant where the motto is "Shut up and shuck," where the superb oysters are fixed thirty different ways and fifteen dollars buys about all anyone can eat. And it has one fly shop—a very good one called Robinson and Sons Outfitters, which is also the place to meet the only two flats guides in town, Tommy and Chris Robinson. As it happens, Tommy sells real estate as well, so he can provide you with the final thing you might come to believe you need in Apalachicola after fishing with him: a house there.

Tommy and his younger brother, Chris, are excellent, widely experienced guides who own a comprehensive knowledge of their wonderfully diverse, year-round, shallow-water fishery. In April and May they can take you to pompano and redfish on the flats and to excellent sight fishing for speckled trout up to six or seven pounds. In June through August they can show you tarpon rolling at the creek mouths early in the morning; large schools of trout and tailing redfish on the flats, along with jack crevalle, pompano, sharks, and cobia; and bluefish and Spanish mackerel around the edges of the flats. In September through December, as the water begins to cool, redfish and trout, many of them big, come into the rivers and creeks and the shallows of the bays to feed on migrating white shrimp, and Chris and Tommy can find you easy sight fishing for them in very shallow water. The area's fine wing shooting for ducks and snipe opens in these months and can be mixed into your fishing by the Robinsons. That shooting continues through the winter, and, except in very cold weather, the redfish are on the flats and fishable January through March and the big, nonmigratory speckled trout move into the river mouths and creeks, making for great plug fishing and easy fly fishing.

All of this plenty can and does result in some true Gone Florida harvests. An Apalachicola fly rod grand slam—not all that usual for a summer day there—is a tarpon, a redfish, a speckled trout, and a tripletail. And one day last December, while Chris and I were releasing redfish after redfish in East Bay under a clearing sky and a reappearing sun that gave the marsh grass a green-gold glow, a friend of Chris's named Nathan stopped shooting teal, gadwall, and mallards just long enough to make a couple of casts out of his duck blind and caught a thirty-four-inch red.

Inside the lagoon the fog had just lifted, the water was still and silver, the rising sun was at our backs, and in the phrase of an old bass fisherman I know, the place "had fish wrote all over it." Chris had just started poling his customized sixteen-foot Alumaweld up the lagoon's south side when a redfish swam up to within four feet of the bow and tailed. I tossed the gold spoon fly to him and he ate it. Egrets flew over. A white heron stalked the far end of the lagoon and a bald eagle circled its nest in a pine on the spit of land between the lagoon and the Gulf. The morning looked like Winslow Homer had painted it. As the sun rose higher, the shallow flat gradually revealed itself, and presently it and the morning were fully achieved, brighter even than their promise. For the next two hours I cast to seven more tailing redfish, caught six, and pulled the hook on the other. For that time, we floated wakeless in four inches of water both down the lagoon and backwards in time, it seemed, through a place where it was as good as you ever dreamed it could be, even in the Gone Florida.

5

UPSTREAM AND DRY

If you happen to be a trout enthusiast you have probably heard of the English chalk streams, and if so, you possibly feel—as I did before I finally visited a number of them—that they are rather like the fishing equivalent of a dusty, leather-bound set of Thomas Carlyle's complete works on your bookshelf: something you should get around to one day, but certainly not before Alaska, Argentina, New Zealand . . . Well, I am here to tell you unequivocally that if you even so much as dabble at fishing for trout, the one place you absolutely must get to is an English chalk stream, preferably at the end of May or beginning of June. Why? Because the trout fishing there and then may very well be the most variously satisfying version of that noble sport to be had anywhere.

There are a number of reasons why this is so, but let us begin with the streams themselves. They take their name from a subsurface band of chalk that runs for some four hundred miles through England, from Dorset in the south to Yorkshire in the north, and was formed by the compacting of shells one hundred million years ago when the British Isles were under three hundred feet of water. Chalk streams are born when rainwater seeps through the chalk into an aquifer and then is forced back to the surface again in the form of springs, which join to become streams. Emerging from the ground at a constant 50 degrees Fahrenheit, filtered by the chalk into a stainless liquid high in alkalinity and rich in nutrients, and running at a more or less constant water level, these streams are nothing less than the world's most perfect trout habitat. They are also hauntingly beautiful and affecting in what the fine English angling writer and chalkstream devotee Charles Rangeley-Wilson calls their "verdant opulence and sedate grandeur." Ambling with bright elegance through undulant green valleys, rich in ranunculus, starwort, and other invertebrate-holding weeds, they are, in Rangeley-Wilson's apt description, "constant, equable, cool, fertile."

There are over one hundred of these magical flowages in England, ranging in size from the jump-overable to ones that are sixty to eighty feet across in places, and in renown from the world famous to ones that are known only to the handful of anglers who fish them. Some are manicured and intensely managed, some are not. Some contain stocked fish, some altogether wild populations. There are brown trout in all of them and, in some, grayling and/or stocked rainbows as well. And on all of them, the fishing rights are privately owned. On a few, public access to those rights is both expensive and exclusive; on others, it is one or the other; and on some, it is neither. For a thorough appreciation of the glories of the chalk streams, a visiting angler should sample one or two from each category, and that it is exactly what Tom Montgomery and I did recently.

We began our tour on the River Test. Located in Hampshire, about an hour and a half southwest of London, it is the long-reigning king of the English chalk streams, both expensive and exclusive, and arguably the most famous trout stream on earth, despite the fact that there are numerous rivers around the world in which more and bigger trout are regularly caught. The Test is uniquely legendary, first because devoted subjects have written about it for over two hundred years, creating a large and effusive literary history that continues today; and second because among its most assiduous chroniclers was a meticulous chap named F. M. Halford who, in the late nineteenth and early twentieth centuries, adopted the river as a laboratory in which to develop and refine the high science and art of dry-fly fishing for trout. In two books and many articles for *The Field* magazine, Halford turned that method of fishing into a sort of cult, with himself as high priest, dispensing not only revolutionary technical information on the dressing and employment of dry flies, but also a body of behavioral rules for that employment: a sort of etiquette, if you will, of on-stream comportment that is still practiced today on the Test (and, to one degree of purity or another, on many of the other chalk streams).

Like many an American first-time visitor to the river, I had certain questions about that etiquette, and I put the most basic of them to Peter Rippin as soon as Tom and I met him on the Boss-ington Estate beat of the Test. Peter is in the pleasant business of providing angling for clients in Iceland, Russia, Cuba, the Sey-chelles Islands, and on the English chalk streams. He had orga-nized the trip for Tom and me, and was on this day guiding us as well. Chipper, keen, well-mannered and turned out, he seemed clearly out of the classic Brit-sportsman mold, and an ideal person to query on the subject.

"Now what is it exactly we do and don't do here?" I asked him. A bit blunt, perhaps, but I had just learned that Bossington Estate belonged to none other than Halford's great-granddaughter and her husband, and I wanted to try to get the thing right.

"Well for a start, you won't need your waders," Peter said. "We fish from a path along the bank. Cast only to rising trout. Up-stream, of course, and only with dry flies. That's about it."

I have one or two troutlaw friends to whom this answer, coming from a young Englishman dressed in plus fours and a necktie, might have been provocation to wader up, plow into the river, and begin flogging a Woolly Bugger downstream. But it sounded like good fun to me. And so it was.

After stringing up a couple of rods, Peter, Tom, and I walked up to the top of our half-mile beat (one of ten, on four miles of the Test owned by the twenty-five-hundred-acre Bossington Estate). We strolled along a wide, neatly mown path beside the bank, looking for rises and enjoying the soul-filling beauties of the Test, exactly as Halford and his friends would have done in 1877. Now, as then, this middle section of the river runs through gentle and verdant farming country; its banks are lined with stately ash, willows, and horse chestnuts; swans, mallards, and tufted ducks ride its unhurried currents above the sweep of dense, viney mats of weed; and its surface is dimpled by rising trout.

In late May and early June, the insect they are mostly rising to is the *Ephemera danica*, referred to throughout England simply as "the mayfly," as that is the month of its celebrated annual appearance on the chalk streams. Both large (about the size of a moth) and evidently toothsome, these bugs are like floating Big Macs, and their profuse hatchings over roughly two weeks cause the normally picky and diffident chalkstream trout to chow down with such adolescent abandon that the period is known as "the duffer's fortnight." It is a little like having two weeks to play St. Andrews during which the holes gobble up your ball, and now as in Halford's time, it is about as much fun as you can have with your plus fours on. You spot a rise, lay your *danica* imitation gently a foot above it, and if your drift is good, a yellow snout rolls up and sips it in.

Fishing in this leisurely, civilized way, Peter and I caught three trout apiece between eleven thirty and one o'clock—vividly col-

ored, hard-fighting browns between a pound and a half and four pounds. We took our lunch of Brie and salmon sandwiches and prosciutto-wrapped pears inside the beat's "lodge," a comfortable building with old rods hung from the ceiling and fishing prints on the walls. And late in the afternoon we walked up to a large, slow pool above a weir and had a couple of hours more of what you will find in the dictionary under "peerless dry-fly fishing."

During a long conversation after lunch, I learned from Brian Parker, for twenty-two years the river-keeper at Bossington, about the management that has been practiced on the Test since Halford's day to create and sustain such brilliant angling. Working seven days a week during the trout season, April 24 through October 10, Brian and his assistant maintain the paths and lodges along the beats, as well as bridges, weirs, benches, and picnic tables. They repair erosion along the river's banks, rake clean the gravel of its spawning beds, and once a year trim back its weeds within the entire four-mile stretch. They "remove unwanted species" (trout eaters such as pike, and cormorants), "discourage" the residency of otters, and closely monitor the beats against poaching human trout eaters. And finally, they raise and stock in the Bossington water some three thousand brown trout and eight hundred rainbows a year, approximately the same number of fish that are caught there annually. On average, three out of four of those caught fish are stocked and one is wild. Peter and I caught some of each, and aside from a subtle difference in the size of their pectoral fins, I found it almost impossible to tell them apart.

With such intensive management and God's own amount of hatching insects, the Bossington water is a very fat paddock for fish and fishermen—producing, according to Brian, wild trout up to six or seven pounds and stocked ones up to ten. I told him I envied him his job and asked how often he fished these pampered and legendary beats himself. He grinned and said, "Years ago when I was a baker I ate myself sick on donuts one day. Haven't eaten one since."

If the Test is the king of English chalk streams, the queen is the Itchen, some of whose beats are even more exclusive and expensive than those on the Test. "Gold dust," is what William Daniel called the one we met him on the next day. "The fishing rights for a beat like this, if they ever came up for sale, would go for a million pounds a mile."

William is in a position to know, being one of the top brokers in England for high-end chalkstream fishing. An ex-London investment banker and lifelong fly fisherman, he started his company, Famous Fishing, thirteen years ago to "access the inaccessible" through his business and fishing contacts. Now he offers that access—on the Test, the Itchen, and a half dozen other chalk streams in Hampshire and Wiltshire—to well-heeled business and private clients at an average of $600 to $700 per rod per day, and at more than $1,000 for certain beats. Like the one we were on.

No more than twenty miles from Bossington and less than ten from the town of Winchester, where lie the bones of Izaak Walton, patron saint of all river anglers, that beat comprised about a mile of the upper Itchen. At thirty feet across, it was half the width of the Bossington water, air clear, home to only wild brown trout, and heart tuggingly, nostalgically beautiful.

"Let the river come to you" is one of the injunctions of chalk-stream fishing. "Study to be quiet," the famous closing words of Izaak Walton's *The Compleat Angler*, is another. I determined to try to do both on this exquisite stream, and so while Tom photographed William's deadly angling below a bridge that halved the beat, I struck off on my own above it. Walking up a path strewn with daisies and buttercups, beside a field with fat sheep grazing, I stopped for minutes at a time and invited the Itchen to visit. Its banks were overhung with willows, and long tendrils of lime-green weeds swayed in its complex currents like a woman's hair. There were very few insects riding that current or in the air, but there seemed to be more Iron Blues than *danica*, so I tied on a small Parachute Adams and waited for rises. When I saw one I would wait again for the fish to come up for a second time before casting.

Over three hours or so I covered less than a quarter of a mile in this way. Hard as I studied to be, I was not entirely quiet and put down a few fish. I hooked and lost a couple, and caught only a half-dozen browns, but I have rarely if ever enjoyed an afternoon of fishing more. I was casting a six-foot three-inch Beasley flame-hardened cane rod, as dainty and comely as the river itself, and on each of the infrequent times it reached out, upstream and dry, to a rising trout, it seemed to put me richly in touch with the river, the chalkstream ethos, and the generations of anglers who had walked slowly, studied the water, and cast to a rise here before. That is not exactly rippin' lips, but if it's not worth a million pounds a mile, I don't know what is.

One of the many pleasures of fishing a sampling of chalk streams during the duffer's fortnight is driving to them through rural England in late spring—through movie-set sixteenth- and seventeenth-century towns with names like Itchen Abbas, Nether Wallop, and Tolpuddle, with their Norman churches and ancient, ale-scented pubs, their thatched-roof houses covered in honeysuckle and climbing roses, their crumbling stone ruins and narrow cobbled streets.

Just outside of one such Cotswold town—that of Bibury, called by William Morris "the most beautiful town in England"—is the Bibury Court Hotel, built in 1633, and set on six acres of wild gardens and lawn, hard by the River Coln. Tom and I checked into it that night after spending a delightful afternoon on a petite chalk stream called the Bourne with Peter Rippin and his brother John. Lovingly immortalized in one of the best of the chalkstream books, *Where the Bright Waters Meet*, by Harry Plunket Greene, the Bourne is both less tended and less mannered than the Test and Itchen, but it is still emphatically chalkstream fishing, with a clear, narrow flow and willow-choked banks that insist on precise casting to finicky, easy-to-spook wild browns up to three pounds.

I could have happily spent a week on it, as I could have on the Coln, where Peter joined us again the next morning, this time with his fiancée, Hannah, to fish a beat he leases just downstream of the Bibury Court. It was the first sunny day we had had. The beat ran through a rich meadow, bright with buttercups and loud with rooks. Peter, Hannah, and I walked along the bank of the Coln, a languid fifty feet across there, chatting and taking turns casting to trout that were feeding on a good hatch of *danica*. If you covered a rising fish without drag, it took the fly every time, and they were strong, chunky browns with a slight rose blush to them. It was as perfect as mornings on a river get, and we topped it off with a long, merry lunch of fish and chips and mugs of Stowford Press cider at The Swan pub in the nearby village of Southrop. Then Tom and I headed south again for Dorset and the rivers Piddle and Frome—"un-bikini-waxed" chalk streams, as they had been described to us by Charles Rangeley-Wilson, who had arranged for our fishing there.

That fishing was just as high quality and interesting as any we had previously had, and the Dorset countryside as soothingly rural, green, and pristine as when Thomas Hardy described it. The waters of the Frome, he wrote in *Tess of the d'Urbervilles*, "were as clear as the pure River of Life shown to the evangelist, rapid as the shadow of a cloud, with pebbly shallows that prattle to the sky all day long." And so they still appeared to Tom and me as we stood on a Christopher Wren bridge eating a local cheddar and watching a piggish brown trout take every *danica* that floated by him—including mine when I finished feeding myself and went down to feed him.

The Piddle was a tiny version of the Frome, difficult, unkempt, and lovely, that holds wild browns up to six pounds. I caught one of about half that size under a willow branch with a side-arm cast after fishing for it for twenty minutes and changing flies four times. And I walked within forty feet of a nearsighted roe deer resting in a meadow on my way back downstream to meet up with Tom and two friends of Charles Rangeley-Wilson who are experts on the unfussy but challenging Dorset chalk streams. Ronnie Butler was a hearty redheaded Scot who owns a map-making company, and Tony Hayter a small, amused-looking academic and biographer of Halford, whose knowledge of British angling and chalk-stream history is encyclopedic. Just having met and having only the Brotherhood of the Angle in common, we stood on a little bridge spanning the Piddle and had an impromptu party for over an hour, discussing various aspects of that brotherhood.

Whether it is on the Test and Itchen, on the less formal streams like the Bourne and Coln, or on the rough and ready ones of Dorset and East Anglia, the duffer's fortnight is a convivial time. From formal lawn parties at the Houghton Club on the Test—at which Prince Charles might be found wandering about with a Pimm's Cup—to a picnic of service-station sandwiches like the one Tom and I had with Peter and John Rippin on the Bourne, anglers from all over Great Britain and other parts of the world engage socially then, as well as on the streams, in a sort of two-week movable feast that has been going on since Halford's day. The men with whom Tom and I shared our time at that feast— Peter, John, William, Ronnie, and Tony—were not only extraordinary anglers, but good-humored, avid, sociable men, gentlemen-sportsmen very much like Halford and his friends, to whom chalk-stream etiquette is nothing more or less than an extension to the streams and the trout that live in them, as well as to other anglers, of the same respect, fairness, and good manners that they practice with each other socially.

On the Itchen, William Daniel had said that what makes chalk-stream fishing still so viable, so *unlike* the molding complete works of Carlyle on your bookshelf, is that while everything else about fly fishing may have changed since the Victorian era, the streams have remained the same, offering the same joys and challenges to a particular type of gracious, self-restrained approach. He could have added that many of the Englishmen who, like himself, are devoted to those streams and their continuing viability, while they might now wear baseball caps instead of tam-o'-shanters, have remained the same as well.

Near the end of our conversation a good trout rose under a willow upstream of the bridge. Tony offered me the go, I offered it to Ronnie, and he back to Tony. Finally Ronnie disappeared into the woods with his rod. Five minutes later, as Tom and I were making plans with Tony to meet the next night at Tony's house for a look at his collection of old chalkstream books, we saw a disembodied fly line suddenly appear over the Piddle, as if from out of one of those books—being cast upstream, of course, and dry.

6

FISHING BABES IN THE EVERGLADES

There we were—three beautiful young women, Val Atkinson, and me, lost in the Everglades on a houseboat that was running out of gas.

Tim, the man who rented us the houseboat, had told us that Pavilion Key was about a two-hour steam south from the marina at Goodland, which should have put us there around eleven thirty in the morning. It was now closing in on two thirty, and we still hadn't come to an island that looked anything like Pavilion appeared to look on the chart. One of the first things you learn about navigating in the Ten Thousand Islands is that all those islands look the same—mangroves and more mangroves, a little beach here and there, and more mangroves. A couple of hours before, we had passed a big island set well offshore, as Pavilion was on the chart, and discussed it, but it seemed the wrong shape for Pavilion, and besides, our fishing guides, Vince Grillo and Mike McComas, were not awaiting us there in their skiffs as Vince assured me they would be, so we puttered on to the south.

"I don't know. I think maybe that's it," Rebel had said at the time, studying the chart.

I had read somewhere not long before that one of the legitimate mental differences between men and women is that women simply do not possess the necessary wiring for navigation, because their prehistoric lot was to stay close to the cave, tending the fire and babies, while men roamed around killing saber-toothed tigers and whatnot. But I didn't want to go into this with Rebel and maybe dampen her sweet, if useless, enthusiasm for helping out, so Val Atkinson, the only other man aboard, and I simply assured her nicely but firmly that she was wrong.

Now that island was but a mote on the northern horizon. To the south lay about 9,750 more islands and then . . . Cuba, maybe? Val worked the chart, while I sat in the captain's chair doing what men do best when they are lost—pressing ahead at top speed, in this case a modest eight knots or so—while keeping one concerned eye on the electronic depth finder and the other on the fuel gauges. We were in six to eight feet of water and it was getting shallower. At three feet, the tubby little houseboat would ground itself and we would be statically rather than dynamically lost, on a chilly, gray, windy afternoon only a few hours before dark in the largest roadless wilderness area in America. That is if we didn't run out of gas first: The gauges on both tanks read less than a quarter full. We could have called someone, of course, on one of the three cell phones we had on board, except that our steadfast pressing ahead had taken us, more than an hour ago, out of cellular range.

All signs, in fact, were pointing grimly toward an adventure terribly other than the one for which I had been preparing my three beauties for weeks with talk of sun-dappled anchorages and the catching of many large fish, and I was grateful that they all seemed nonmutinously, even agreeably, occupied—Heather and Greta with making sandwiches and organizing our stores in the small galley, and Rebel with continuing to try, touchingly, to help unlose us.

She was standing beside me glassing the water and the islands to the south with a pair of binoculars. "I'm sorry we're off to such a rough start, Reb," I said to this lovely and indomitable pal of mine. I wanted to be upbeat. "The Coast Guard will probably find us eventually."

"Who needs 'em?" snorted Rebel. "Besides, like they used to say on *Northern Exposure*, "It's not the thing you fling, but the fling itself.""

I contemplated this piece of news to me, looking in it for a nugget of the kind of Zennish feminine wisdom I had hoped to mine on this trip.

"It's not the what, now . . . ?"

"I see a channel marker," said Rebel, who had not taken the binoculars away from her face in over fifteen minutes. "And it has a number on it." She grabbed the chart away from Val and found the numbered channel marker. "Here we are," she said, marking the spot with an X. Then she measured a mile with her thumb and forefinger from the scale at the bottom of the chart and hopped the two fingers from the X back north to Pavilion Key, struggling valiantly against the primordial mental deficiency of her gender. "About twelve miles south of that big island I told you guys was the one. Turn around."

Vince Grillo and Mike McComas were waiting for us in their imperiously nimble little skiffs on the inshore side of said big island—where they had been when we passed it too far offshore to see them the first time—and they led us to our anchorage up the Chatham River. It was nearly five o'clock when we got the house-boat secured fore and aft in a fine, buxom curve of the river. The weather was clearing, the wind dropping, and my girls were ready to go fishing.

Vince asked me what I wanted to do about getting more gas for the boat.

"Don't worry about gas," said Greta, who was standing with her hands on her hips in the stern looking down at him. She had just put a big wad of Skoal under her lip and now spit tobacco juice out over the rail. "Girls can *always* get gas. The question is how many fish are we going to catch with you guys?"

"Don't know, Gretchen," said Vince, a grandfatherly type who seemed a little rattled by the Skoal. "Fish are almost as undependable as women."

This earned him a chorus of boos.

"And it's Greta," added my daughter, "not Gretchen."

Heather was standing in the bow of the houseboat in a T-shirt and bikini bottom, warming up an eight-weight fly rod.

Mike McComas said, "Hey Vince, we got one here who can cast."

"You got one here who can *fish*," said Heather.

"*That*," said Mike, already showing somewhat more than a spark of interest, "remains to be seen."

One afternoon not long ago, having nothing better to do, I calculated that I have spent over a decade of the days of my life, somewhere around four thousand of them, whiling away time in the out of doors with rod or gun. Though no doubt it should be, that fact is not shocking to me; what is shocking—because on the whole I much prefer women to men—is to realize that fewer than a hundred of those days have been spent in the company of females.

My wife doesn't hunt or fish and neither do most of the women I know. Most of the women of my generation and older, particularly ones from the South, where I live, consider those pursuits unladylike and riddled with inferior bathrooms, and will do them grudgingly only to please or keep their husbands, or as a way of being with men when other women are not. There are exceptions, of course—I think of my beautiful and spirited friend Peggy Pepper, who was still avidly pursuing bobwhite quail in her late seventies; of Heidi Kulish who outfished me and Russell Chatham one day on a Montana spring creek, and wrote to me about nothing but trout when she was dying of brain cancer; about the elegant Joan Wulff, and the tireless Suzie Moore who will do it with you, whatever it is, until you keel over—but these are exceptions that prove the rule.

I know lots of women in my daughter's generation, however—postfeminist, male-unreliant, kickass women—including my daughter herself, who are passionate about fishing and/or hunting, who are at least as competent at them as most men, and who don't give a rat's ass who knows it. On my too-infrequent outings with such women, I have not only enjoyed myself more than I do with all but a handful of males but have sensed some difference both in what they bring to fishing and hunting and what they get out of them that seems to me as fresh, poignant, and mysteriously desirable as the smell of wild roses.

For three months last winter after an operation, I found myself orthopedically confined twenty-four hours a day by a brace that stretched from my mid-back to my knee. Being in the thing felt to me like being sent back to military school, and I chafed. In February, after dutifully doing nothing that was fun for over two months and still in the brace, I accepted an invitation to go chukar and pheasant shooting at a lodge in Idaho. Both the shooting and the lodge were excellent, and the ten or twelve other men staying at and running the place were all perfectly nice; and yet after only two days of all-male hunting lodge humor, attitudes, and conventions, I felt like I was slogging through a deepening and endless bog—one I had plunged into as a stripling and had loved most of

my life, gamboling around in it like a sika deer, but recently had begun to find as confining and oppressive as the brace I was wearing.

When I got home I told my wife at dinner that after the brace came off in a few weeks I wanted to take a different kind of fishing trip.

"And what kind of fishing trip could that possibly be at this point?" she wondered.

"I want to go off on a houseboat into the Everglades with three smart, articulate, beautiful young women who fish like ospreys."

"Uh huh."

"I mean it."

"Was it something I said, something I did?" asked Patricia, still not taking me seriously.

"One of them would be Greta, of course. Rebel, maybe. Maybe Heather Andrews. I want to learn what's different about the way these young women fish and just *are* in the outdoors. I have this feeling that . . ."

"It's okay," Patricia interrupted. "I think it's actually sort of a sweet idea. I think you'll learn a lot."

"And they will too, of course . . ."

"Do you know what I hope, though?" asked Patricia

"No."

She smiled. "I hope they're all three PMS-ing."

Greta and I flew to Fort Myers on April 17, picked up Val Atkinson there, and drove south of Naples to a marina in a place called the Isles of Capri. As mentioned, the weather was less than perfect—windy and gray, with temperatures barely cracking 60. "This is South Florida at its absolute worst," the rental car agent had said. "We just don't have cold fronts this late in the spring. It's bizarre."

"Uh-uh," said Greta, whose angling sorties to good-weather destinations have so often coincided with awful weather that her nickname in our family is "Cold Front."

"Not to us it's not."

Greta grew up between an older and a younger brother, both of whom were good athletes. She has played men's games with men all her life, and not off the women's tee. In 1992 she won the Women's World Extreme Snowboarding Championship is Valdez, Alaska, and beat a number of men in the competition. She is an accomplished Alpinist, founder of the Wild Women Snowboard

Camps, owner of a couple of snowboard first descents, an ac-
claimed singer-songwriter, an ex-television sports host, and skilled
fly angler who has not given up a dram of femininity in being any
of these things. If it sounds a bit like I'm bragging here, I am. I
have an extraordinary daughter, a creature who probably would
have been impossible at any age before this one, and whose company, outdoors and indoors, I enjoy as much as anyone's on earth.
She *can* be snippy though.

Looking for the first time at our home away from home for the
next few days, she said, "This is disgusting. Do you know how '70s
this thing is? As '70s as bellbottoms."

"Nehru jackets," agreed her friend Heather Andrews, who had
joined up with us at the marina.

Heather and Greta met when they both lived in Jackson Hole,
Wyoming, in the early '90s. Heather was married for five years to
one of the best trout guides in that town and she and her husband
ran a bonefish lodge in the Bahamas for a year where Heather fell
for fly fishing. Now she was teaching it at The Whitetail Fly Fishing School in Mercersburg, Pennsylvania, and fishing every
chance she got. Her skill at the sport, along with her tendency to
practice it in a bikini and her considerable comeliness had landed
her photograph in a number of national magazines, including
Sports Afield, whose first-ever female cover shot of her casting to a
bonefish in trademark attire is now pinned to God-only-knows-
how-many fishing camp walls. This does not bother Heather.

The forty-foot Holiday Mansion houseboat called the "Lookin'
Good" that she and Greta were insulting was tan with orange
carpets, a bit squat and lumpy, perhaps, but rather cheerful and
staunch looking, I thought—even if it did have a broken starter. So
did its sister boat, tied on the other side of the dock, and they were
the only two houseboats that Houseboat Rentals of Florida had
left. The owner of the boats, Steve Meek, was working on one of

the starters; Tim Gary, proprietor of the rental company, had driven into town to try to replace the other one. These two men were in their fifties, good-natured transplants from the North to whom life in South Florida seemed to be largely about working happily on broken boats and, in Tim's case, selling a little real estate, and more or less round-the-clock beer.

"Don't worry," said Steve Meek, "we'll have one of them fixed for you to take down to Goodland before dark. Go get your groceries and we'll have 'er up and running by the time you get back."

They did, to our surprise; and after a quick crash course from Steve on the boat's various systems, we steamed out for Goodland, home of the Buzzard Lope and jump-off for the Ten Thousand Islands. Tim was at the wheel. For the hour or so duration of the trip, he brandished a beer, kept his eyes glued to Greta and Heather, and instructed Val and me with what was left of his attention on the operation of the houseboat.

"Did I remember to tell you guys about the tub switch?" he'd say.

"I think Steve told us about that," I'd say. "Or was that the pump-out switch for the head, Val?"

"Steve showed us where the fuses are," Val would say. "I remember that. What switch is it again?"

The boat had a tiny head with a toilet and shower/tub, a tiny bunk room with two bunks where all three girls were going to sleep, a wheel room with a couch that made into a bed, a step-down galley and dining room with another convertible couch, small aft and foredecks, and a roomy upper deck and flying bridge. Moreover, it had a generator, two air conditioners, a thermostat, bilge pump blowers, depth finders, an emergency gas tank, cut-out switches, filters, circuit breakers, shut-offs, a stove, refrigerator, and TV/VCR, a hot-water heater, cell phone, floodlights, toolbox, binoculars, and charts—the whereabouts and operations of all of which were still largely in question when Tim docked us at Goodland and quit the boat.

About an hour later Steve called and told me over the barely working cell phone how to turn off some "very important switch" in the engine compartment that he had neglected to mention. I told him that the girls seemed to have stopped up the shower. "Try the . . . ," he said and the phone cut out.

While Val and I were finding and turning off the very important switch, Tim showed back up in a festive mood with, of all things, a beer in his hand, and after he unplugged the shower filter we offered to take him to dinner in town, because none of us was in the mood to risk encouraging anything else on board to quit working by cooking.

At Little Bar in Goodland (population five hundred) there was a country band, a dining room, and a bar area crowded with crab fisherman in white rubber boots and a big group of matrons from Marco Island on a high school reunion fling. We ate in the dining room while Tim put back a truly remarkable number of gin and tonics and told us about the huge parties held every Sunday just down the street at Stan's Idle Hour waterfront bar. The partying started at noon with the singing of the national anthem and ended around seven. There would be as many as three thousand people on a nice day, he said, coming from all over South Florida—bums next to millionaires, old beat-up jon boats tied up at Stan's dock next to cigarette boats and yachts. Tim said he figured it was the best party in Florida, and maybe the most unusual as well because of the Buzzard Lope.

"Which is what?" asked Heather.

"Sort of a dance, I guess you'd call it," Tim said. "During the Mullet Festival one year, Stan noticed that all the women in the bar just sat around doing nothing while their husbands were in the mullet-fishing contest, so he wrote this song called the 'Buzzard

Lope' and got the women to dance to it. Now they do it every Sunday on the outdoor stage. There's *hundreds* of them out there waving their feet in the air."

"Doing *what*?" Greta asked him.

"They lie down on their backs on the stage and jerk their feet around in the air like a buzzard hit on the side of the road. Every-body does it a little different." Greta and Heather turned their blonde, Teutonic heads to look at each other, and I swear it sounded like the band might have lapsed for a moment into "The Ride of the Valkyries." "If you girls were going to be here on Sunday, you could give 'er a try," Tim said.

"I don't think it's us," said Greta.

"We'd rather beat all the men in the mullet-fishing contest," said Heather.

Rebel Kelley, our last crew member, arrived sometime after midnight from New Orleans, and the next morning we left the marina at Goodland at nine thirty and cruised down the Marco River and out into the Gulf for the easy two-hour run southeast to Pavilion Key.

"How will we recognize the island?" Val asked when we were telling Tim good-bye.

"Oh, you can't miss it. Just call if anything goes wrong. But it won't."

Once we finally got out in the skiffs with Vince and Mike that first afternoon, the fishing was slow, but the babes and I enjoyed it anyway. In the boat with Vince and Val and Greta, I lay on the seat in front of the console and watched my daughter knocking the eyes out of mangrove pockets with a steamer, in a variation of the bass fly rodding she's been doing since she was a little girl, and was a contented man.

After a while, Greta hooked a fish that made a strong first run. "Is that a shnook?" she asked Vince.

"A jack," said Vince. "Keep your tip up."

"It's called a snook, Greta," I told her. "Not a shnook."

"What I want is a big shnook," she said, reefing on the jack. "I've never caught one before."

Vince was a gentlemanly retired suburban real estate developer who had moved to the Everglades town of Chokoloskee from Colorado eight years before and started guiding to give himself something to do. A few minutes after Greta caught the jack, he and Val and I were talking about the trout lakes in Browning, Montana, near where Vince lives in the summer. "Could you guys not talk so loud?" Greta asked us. "You could be spooking the shnook."

"You gotta like the attitude," said Vince.

Around seven o'clock, Vince and Mike planed up out of the bay we had been fishing and ran back to the "Looking' Good" through a series of little lakes and mangrove-tousled creeks, putting up egrets and cormorants into an oranging sky. And after they dropped us off and started their thirty-minute run back to Chokoloskee, we had all we could see and hear of the Everglades profoundly to ourselves on a beautiful, clearing evening.

Maybe it was the solitude that encouraged a lively volubility in the girls after we had cooked and eaten dinner and washed the dishes; or maybe it didn't need encouraging. After agreeing on Katharine Hepburn as the patron saint of this trip and the coolest woman ever, they moved on to how they felt about the turning over to a man any of the remarkably autonomous control all three of them presently had over their lives. Greta and Heather each had boyfriends and no wish to marry anytime soon; Rebel was within weeks of wedding an excellent man named Charlie, thus dashing for good the hopes and dreams of hundreds of guys, young and old, all over south Louisiana. Surprisingly, all three of the babes said they had no problem with a man running the show—so long as it was the right man.

Rebel: "I'm telling you, Charlie is the fucking *man*. He's got the wheel. But the guy's got to earn that. He has to be man enough."

Heather: "Or have a big enough check book."

Greta: "To me he has to *respect* you—who you are and what you want to do with your life. The only kind of men who deserve being the boss are the ones who don't want to be—the guys who really respect women."

"Like Bill Clinton," I offered disingenuously, loosing a torrent of vitriol over the line, "I did *not* have sexual relations with that woman"—over the chickenshit hairsplitting of it; over the arrogance of the phrase "that woman," the lowlife *soullessness* of it.

And on that very same good-old-boy sense of the value and usefulness of women, Rebel had an illustrative Cajun joke: "Pierre and Boudreau are fishing partners. Pierre comes to Boudreau's house one day and says, 'Boudreau, I have some bad news and some good news. The bad news is your wife Maureen drowned. The good news is she's got fourteen of the finest blue crabs on her you ever saw and we're gonna run her again tomorrow'."

Greta: "Exactly! Men are straight lines, woman are circles. A man is like, okay, here's a problem, what's the quickest unemotional way to solve it. Women are all about bringing things around. Our bodies were built to serve somebody else. I have to work all the time to be good and fair to myself."

Heather: "We're built to be a vessel, but I resent the fact that we have to rely on men to make it happen."

Greta: "You don't, Heather. All you need for that's a turkey baster."

At some point I suggested, perhaps smugly, that what all of them seemed to want were the qualities more often found in older men than younger ones.

"Not me," said Heather. "I want hair."

"But not on the back," said Rebel. That's my absolute first rule—N.H.O.B. No hair on the back!"

Before they went to bed, Heather couldn't find her hairbrush and asked if either of the other girls had a pink hairbrush.

"I have a black one," said Rebel.

"Never mind," Heather said. "I can't really brush with anything but a pink one." Then she asked Greta, with whom she was sharing one of the two bunks below, if Greta would "spoon" with her when they got in bed. The little head, when I brushed my teeth, was full of eye-makeup remover, hair conditioner, moisturizer, something called thigh cream . . . I went to sleep on one of the pull-out couches, wondering if Val Atkinson, who has been on more exotic fishing trips than anyone I know, felt as utterly far-flung on this one as I did.

The next morning the boat's batteries were dead. We got the water running and the toilet flushing with the generator, which would also eventually recharge the boat's batteries, but the generator ran on gas and we were just slap out of that. Which I relayed to Tim when I somehow managed to get him on the cell phone.

"Don't worry. I'll bring out some gas tomorrow. I'll be there at noon sharp."

"Why do you think the batteries died?" I asked him.

"The fridge runs them down overnight. Didn't Steve tell you that? Just turn off the fridge before you go to bed. Look, I've got to go show some people some real estate. See you tomorrow at noon."

It was a sunny day, if still cool and breezy, on the back end of Greta's cold front. The two fishing guides arrived at nine wearing pile jackets, not a good sign when you're snook fishing. Rebel and Greta went with Vince, Heather and I with Mike, and Val with Bill Wells, a retired dentist, in Bill's jon boat. Again, the fishing was slow, but around eleven o'clock Greta caught a bragging-size nine-pound snook. Though the fish was of a legal length to keep, nine out of ten of Mike's and Vince's clients would have released it. Greta was the tenth.

"Are you kidding? I'm going to eat the sucker," she told Vince when he asked her if she was sure she didn't want to let the snook go. She wouldn't even put it back into the water while it was still hooked so Val could get a picture of it being brought aboard.

"Do you want to see my shnook?" she hollered across the bay we were all fishing to Mike and Heather and me.

"We'll see it at lunch," I shouted back, and Greta did not let us forget to do that when we went in to a little beach an hour and a half later to eat. While we were there, a square-jawed, squinty-eyed geezer with a pipe paddled up in a well-loaded canoe. He was a retired ship's captain on a fourteen-day solo paddle from Flamingo to Everglade City, through the lonely heart of the Everglades, and our beach was where he was planning to spend the night. He did not seem happy to see three boats there until he spotted the girls, and then his eyes widened in a sort of merry, old-salt astonishment. I told him they were women who had left their husbands in Cleveland and that Val and I had picked them up in a bar in Tampa and brought them out here on our yacht.

"Some yacht," said Rebel. "We shoulda stayed in Cleveland."

"Do you want to see my schnook?" Greta asked him.

Chewing on a piece of jerky for his lunch, the hard old fellow told me that paddling back and forth alone through the Everglades was his life. But a few minutes later, as he stood on the beach smoking his pipe and watching the fishing babes depart, he looked like he might have been ready for a change.

It warmed up that afternoon and Heather stripped down to her renowned bikini. I lounged on the console seat watching her fly rod the bank from the bow with considerable panache and listening to her conversation with Mike. Through the day that conversation had grown more animated and personal on both their parts and was now on an easy level of intimacy that very few male sports would have achieved with a guide, even one as outgoing and likable as Mike McComas, in a week of fishing. Perhaps it had something to do with the view he was enjoying from the poling platform over the engine, but Mike grew more and more expansive as the afternoon wore on, though he stopped short of taking off his own shirt when Heather invited him to.

He told her about moving down to South Florida from Ohio twenty-four years ago; about tiring of the restaurant business in Naples and deciding to get his guide's license a little over a year ago. She told him about selling radio advertising and running the bonefish lodge in the Bahamas with her ex. He told her he'd never been married, just never found the right girl, and Heather said she was surprised at that.

There were big schools of mullet wrinkling the surfaces of the tannic water, ibis and ospreys overhead, and the wall-to-wall clickings and meshings of intertwined life that make up the unique hum of the Everglades. Heather caught a snook and then another one; she moved a number of big fish that were unhungry in the cold-front chilled water; and she paid attention to catching and not catching, where she was and what else was there, and the conversation she was having with Mike on just the right frequencies.

"Good *cast*," Mike told her toward the end of the afternoon. "*Beautiful* cast."

"If you could just end that with 'baby,' it'd be better," Heather said and smiled slightly.

"What was that?" asked Mike.

"Do you think you could make that, 'Beautiful cast, baby'?"

"Hey, no *problem*, baby," said Mike. "Here I am trying to keep some professional distance . . ."

"I threw all that out the window hours ago," Heather told him.

Thirty minutes later, Mike said, "Wind it up, baby. It's time to go home."

After swimming and bathing in the Chatham River and watching a fat red sunset from the upper deck, we ate the ceviche that Greta had made with the stomach meat of her snook and then fillets of the fish, cooked in tin foil with chopped onion, lemons, and tomatoes, along with corn on the cob, salad, and a bottle or two of Chardonnay.

The houseboat had run out of fresh water for cooking, showering, and washing dishes, but nobody cared. The girls washed the dishes in salt water, then sat cross-legged on the couches spoofing on the picture of a male model in *Vanity Fair*, to whom Greta had assigned a life history, the name 'Tony,' and a torrid but hopeless relationship with herself. As she elaborated on why it could never work out with Tony, she painted her toenails a burnt umber color and Heather braided her hair in pigtails. Vince had told me that morning that he had gone home the night before and told his wife that he was fishing with three women who were wannabe men. I told him I didn't think he had that quite right.

The next morning the houseboat's batteries were dead again, though we had turned off the fridge the night before. We didn't even bother to charge them since we would be coming back to the boat at noon to meet Tim with the gas. Mike arrived early to take Heather and Val into the outside water of the Gulf in hopes of finding hungrier snook and maybe even some tarpon. Heather was just a tad grumpy because of the hour and said, "Maybe I'm tired of being a fishing babe. Maybe I want to lie around the boat and be a glamour babe today."

"Get in the boat, baby," Mike told her.

When the other two guides arrived at nine, Rebel went out plug casting with Bill, and Greta and I spent the morning with Vince, who had to work hard at trying to find us fish. "Hey," Greta told him, "you haven't been on trips with me and my Dad before. At least it's not *hailing* on us like it did in Exuma."

We were back at the houseboat by noon, as was the other skiff, but there was no sign of Tim. Not by twelve thirty, or one, or one thirty either. We turned on the generator and hoped (a) that it would charge the batteries enough to get the boat going by our three thirty departure time, and (b) that there was enough gas to do that and still make it out of the river to open water. When our diminishing options started causing me to feel a little testy, Rebel reminded me that it was the fling not the thing, or however it went, and that sounded about right. So we left Bill Wells with the houseboat just in case Tim showed up, and went fishing—Heather and Mike, of course, and Greta, Rebel, Val, and I with Vince.

I met Rebel Ann Kelly a few years ago in Louisiana on another fishing trip, an all-male one. In her capacity as assistant director and information officer for the Louisiana Chapter of the Coastal Conservation Association, she joined that trip for a few days and illuminated its progress like a headlamp in a coal mine. In addition to being very good at her job, working to preserve and protect Gulf Coast gamefish populations, Rebel proved to be resourceful, intelligent, untiringly upbeat, funny, loyal, shrewd, perspicacious at finding and having fun, lionhearted, and a great dancer. Other than that and her wonderful looks, she struck me as just another run-of-the-mill female, but one I wanted to get to know anyway.

Like Heather and Greta, Rebel has become a poster girl for the new outdoors enthusiasm among young women: She had been pictured on the cover of *Louisiana Sportsman* magazine and was a catalog model for the Orvis Company. Like the other two babes,

she was introduced to fishing by a man who lives and breathes it—
her fiancé, Charlie—and had come to feel as passionately about it
as he does. And also like Heather and Greta, she fishes with skill,
perseverance, and brio.

Standing on the bow of Vince's skiff, she was deadly with her
custom-made spinning rod, laying a spoon into pockets in the
mangroves little bigger than an egg, finessing rather than muscling
the casts, attending to each one with focus but without the blin-
dering, anticipatory intent and ambition that so many males, including myself, tend to bring to our flings. She and Val and I each
had a few shots at big snook in the couple of hours we fished, but
all of them had lockjaw. When I found myself almost as serene
about that fact as Rebel was, I felt that perhaps I was making some
progress in my search for feminine insight. And Rebel confirmed
that feeling a few minutes later.

Val was casting my fly rod. "Nice outfit," he said to me, "Did
you say it's nine and a half feet?"

"Yeah," I told him. "And I really like that extra six inches."

"You sound just like a woman," Rebel said.

When we got back to the houseboat at three thirty, there was a
flashy speedboat-looking thing tied up alongside it and Tim was on
board helping himself to our gin with a buddy of his named Junior
who was, said Tim, a retired millionaire. Tim and Junior had
gassed up the boat and appeared to be as glad to see us as we were
to see them.

"Everything went fine, right?" Tim said.

"Uhh. Few little things. We ran out of water," I told him.

"Women," said Tim, with his canny, booze-mellowed eyes on
them. "Women use a lot of water."

"You're a little late," I mentioned.

"My boat wouldn't start. You know how boats are."

We pulled the anchors and told Vince good-bye. Unanxious to leave, Mike offered to help Tim and Junior lead us out of the river and into open water, noting that the two gents in the speedboat might perhaps, in their gaiety, misplace the channel on the way out. Before we left, Greta, wearing her bikini, jumped down into Tim's boat to have a look around, then climbed back onto the houseboat. Watching her, Junior made a wistful and appreciative little noise.

"Al*right*, Junior," said Heather. "You don't even *need* Viagra to appreciate that, do you buddy?"

"Nope," Junior concurred.

A couple of hours later we anchored up in the lee of an island in the Gulf just off a white beach where hundreds of horseshoe crabs were mating in the sand. Tim and Junior had roared away, and Mike had hugged Greta and Rebel, and Heather in particular. "Your girls fish better than 70 percent of my male clients," he told them, and harder than 80 percent."

"You're probably not going to forget this trip soon, are you, Mike?" Val asked him.

"Are you kidding? I've just come off of two weeks of fat doctors from Wisconsin and have more of 'em coming up. I'm *never* going to forget this trip," Mike said, and with a last wave to Heather took his unhappy leave.

The CD player was going strong. We swam and bathed off the little beach and Rebel shaved her legs on the fantail. Greta lolled in the water and allowed that she was tired. "It's the sun," Rebel told her. "This sun 'll knock your dick in the dirt."

It was a balmy, pluperfect evening: pelicans on the wing, a stagy sunset, X-rated crabs on the beach. With pork tenderloins on the grill and pasta in the pot, the fishing babes put on dresses for the trip's last night and Rebel made sundowners out of rum and pineapple chunks that were so good, she said, "It'll make you want to slap your mama."

After dinner the babes discovered a tape of *Grease*, their all-time favorite movie, they agreed—and played it on the VCR. I remember that some girl in a red wig said to Olivia Newton John, "Men are rats . . . and there are *fleas* on rats," at which my three lovelies cracked up; and that John Travolta turned out to be in fact not a rat but a good guy and a Hollywood-version real man after all.

And what, in their opinions, was a "real man"? I asked the girls after the movie. They were sucking on lollipops at the time, their legs tucked under them on the couch, looking drop-dead in their dresses.

Rebel: "Charlie. Somebody who will stop the fishing boat and watch the dolphins playing, who knows it's not all about the action."

Heather: "Someone who'll show you his vulnerability. Someone who knows exactly who he is and allows you to be who you are. And a man who really loves women and doesn't just pretend to."

Greta: "And appreciates the feminine side of himself. Like some tough old farmer guy who understands calving. The good kind of toughness in a man is suppleness. It's not an idea or a fact. It's organic—managing, coping, not coming apart in the crunch like a two-dollar suitcase."

Heather: "Yeah, I want that. And a guy who can be your best friend as well as your lover."

Rebel: "What I want is for Charlie to let me do what I want to do but by God still open my door *every* time."

Greta: "And I want a man who can out-fish me, out-snowboard me, take care of the kids, recite a little William Blake, describe something to me so that it is so lucid I am moved to tears by his mind, who has charisma, tremendous energy, who's great looking, nice buns . . ."

"Somebody just like Tony," said Heather.

"Right on," said Rebel. "Why not go for it *all*, honey?"

Before they went to bed, I asked them what they were afraid of.

Heather said, "My biggest fear is becoming fearful. Don't you get more fearful as you get older?"

Greta said, "The only thing that terrifies me is being bored. Being stagnant. Not being able to be a pioneer."

Rebel said, "Oh, I don't know. Nothing, I guess."

And that nothing included apparently a broken generator the next morning. Val and I both tried the thing and it wouldn't turn on. It didn't even make a noise. Without the generator, because the batteries were dead again, the boat wouldn't start and we were once again potential alligator bait, not to mention—depending, as we would be, on Tim to come and get us—without any hope of making our planes that afternoon.

"What do you think is wrong with it?" I asked Val.

"Just broken, I guess."

"Yeah." And having exhausted our mechanical ingenuity, we wrote the generator off and had another cup of instant coffee.

Five minutes later Rebel came up from below, stretching. "Good morning," she said. "Why do you boys look so glum?"

"Generator's broken," said Val. "We can't start the engines."

Rebel walked over to the switch, gave it a friendly, feminine little wiggle and the ingratiating, doubtless lovesick generator *leaped* obediently to life. "There you go," said Rebel, and went into the galley to start breakfast.

We had a flawless morning for the boat ride back to Goodland: blue skies, warm sun, a merry little breeze. Val and I sat up on the flying bridge running the boat and navigating, of course. But with

Rebel nearby. In excellent spirits, she and the other two babes were stretched out on the upper deck sunbathing. One of Greta's CDs was playing at volume. The little houseboat seemed to cha-cha along over the bright sea.

"Do we *have* to go home?" asked Heather, turning over on her back. "Why couldn't we just get Tim and Junior to keep bringing us more gas and go on to Mexico? And you guys could do another story: 'Fishing Babes in Mexico.'"

It sounded like a splendid idea to me, and I said so. Over the past few days I hadn't fished much and honestly can't at this moment remember what I caught. But I felt wonderful: replete, temporarily but precisely resolved—the way the terminations of only the very best trips can make you feel. In point of fact, I felt like singing.

"Hey, Gret," I yelled over her voice on the CD. "How does that song go?"

"*What* song, Dad?"

"You know the one. Sort of the fishing babes' anthem."

Greta almost always *does* know what I mean. She laughed. "Oh you mean the *hokey* one." Then she sang it. I sang along.

> *I can bring home the bacon . . .*
> *Fry it up in a pan . . .*
> *And never, ever let you forget you're a man . . .*

7

TURNING TEN AGAIN

Over the three previous days in Havana I had become fondly accustomed to feeling locked in a 1950s time warp. Now, it was nothing less than thrilling to find myself fishing in one too.

I was standing in the tiny V-shaped bow of a ten-foot fiberglass pirogue kind of thing. It was old and green, its only engine a wiry little guy in the stern named Lazaro, who was poling the miniature skiff along at a handsome clip with a weathered driftwood stick. We were surrounded by half a million hectares of virgin swampland and over a hundred thousand acres of prime bonefish stomping grounds. Somewhere out there, each in a similar skiff, were *mi amigos*, Ethan, Des, Richard, and Eric. But *no one else*. Not another boat of any kind. The nearest condos and Jet Skis were over a hundred miles away in Key West. And as Lazaro poled us up to the first flat of the morning, putting to wing a pair of white ibis, I literally felt ten years old again.

It was at that age when I caught my first bonefish, in June of 1952, fishing with my father out of the old Walker's Cay Club in the Bahamas. We fished with spinning rods, hooks baited with conch, and no sunscreen from a rowboat poled by a guide with a drift-wood stick. The club was owned by a friend of my father's who made helicopters. It slept six or eight people in concrete bunk rooms. Dinner at night was eaten with the guides and consisted of whatever fish you or someone else had caught that day. The generator went off at ten, and you shared the little saltwater pool with a three-foot blacktip shark named Hank.

These days such a place would not pass for what is known as a "bonefish destination." The myriad of these in the Bahamas, Mexico, Belize, Venezuela, and the Seychelles are, almost with exception these days, stylish lodges featuring "island gourmet cuisine" and a choice of wines with dinner, and frequented by an international army of garrulous fly rodders in Orvis, Patagonia, and ExOfficio uniforms. To be sure, since 1952 I have put in more of my own tours of duty at these places than is seemly, and have enjoyed most of them and come to love a few. Moreover, I prefer a nice meal over a nasty one every bit as much as Auden did, and I have no problem with showers that work and overdesigned $40,000 bat-out-of-hell skiffs. But after you have been to enough modern bonefish destinations they can all seem to blur together into a characterless if-it's-November-it-must-be-Abaco whole; and more than once over the years I have longed to pass through a worm-hole back to something like the Walker's Cay Club—a place with enough unmistakable *there* there to make it impossible to wake up and have to spend a moment remembering where exactly you are in Bonefish Nation.

The Zapata Peninsula is located on Cuba's southwest coast, some two and a half hours drive from Havana. At 4,520 square kilometers, it is the largest maritime wilderness area in Cuba and, by far, the largest swampland in the Caribbean. The peninsula is very lightly inhabited by humans, and a chunk of it the size of Delaware, known as the Zapata Swamp National Park, is protected from poaching and commercial exploitation. That protection notwithstanding, if this jewel of a bird-watching, diving, beaching, and fishing resource were anywhere else in the Caribbean, it would be covered up with marinas, resorts, and angling lodges. But it has the good luck to be located in Cuba—which under Castro has the perhaps surprising distinction of having locked up 22 percent of its land under some form of environmental protection, among the highest of any nation; and where (to date) there is little if any capitalistic incentive to develop it, let alone the infrastructure necessary to do so.

Other than a bit of salt mining and sugar milling of centuries ago (and the hosting in 1961 of the failed U.S.-backed invasion of the Bay of Pigs, which forms the peninsula's eastern boundary), nothing much has happened in the Zapata since the Taino Indians owned it in 1100 AD. As a result, its pine and mangrove forests, swamps, and estuaries are bursting with resident and migrant

birds (more than 190 species, and 18 of Cuba's 21 endemic ones are found there), mammals, and reptiles—including a population of crocodiles said to be far more numerous than human inhabitants. And, as you may have guessed, there are fish there as well.

Sport fishing was first allowed in the park in 1994. That was a decade after it opened, and the intervening ten-year ban on any kind of fishing allowed gamefish stocks to recover from commercial overharvesting to full carrying capacity. There continues to be almost no commercial fishing in the park, and the sport fishing there is operated as a strictly regulated government concession from two locations. One of these is the beautiful Hatiguanico River; the other is Las Salinas—a remote little launch site on the peninsula's south coast that accesses the vast system of flats there, as well as a barrier island about an hour offshore whose five fish-rich transecting channels are known as the Bocas.

Together, the flats, the Bocas, and the river make up one of the most varied, shallow saltwater fisheries on earth—offering up bonefish, permit, tarpon, snook, cubera snapper, jacks, and other species. It is also one of the most pristine. The government allows only eight anglers a day to fish out of Las Salinas, and because there are more than one hundred thousand acres of flats there accessible only by poled pirogue, huge areas of those flats are never even seen, much less fished.

There is no "bonefish destination" in the Zapata. What there is instead is a funky little accommodation called the Hotel Playa Larga, in the village of the same name. The hotel is right on the Bay of Pigs and its pretty white sand beach is one of two onto which the hapless Cuban exiled invaders spilled on April 16, 1961—fifty years and one day before Des Fitzgerald, Ethan

Hawke, our host and outfitter Richard French, photographer Eric Kiel, and I arrived.

There was no shark in the pool at the Hotel Playa Larga, but there was plenty of *there* there: a multitude of festive rural Cubans of all ages frolicking in the ocean and drinking cerveza; antique American cars parked side by side with mules at the entry to the beach; and a nearby baseball diamond aswarm with grazing goats, chickens, and pigs. The hotel itself consisted of an office/bar/dining-room building and forty-one cement bungalows painted in assertive pastels, each with air conditioning, two comfortable beds, and a wide tile porch on which to enjoy a predinner mojito and an after-dinner rum and cigar. In all, it was not perhaps every bone-fish soldier's cup of tea, but I was powerfully smitten with the place; and I went to bed that first night already in the grip of the happy, transporting *nostalgie de la jeunesse* that owned me for the next four days.

The following morning, after a good breakfast at the hotel of fruit, cheese omelets, and electrifying Cuban coffee, we boarded our chartered bus for the fifty-minute drive to Las Salinas. That drive takes you through the village of Playa Larga; past monuments marking the spots where individual Cuban soldiers died during the Bay of Pigs invasion; and past the ever-present little groups of people standing around chatting on the streets, and others on bicycles, in horse-drawn buggies, oxcarts, and the occasional two-toned Ford Fairlane or fin-tailed Cadillac that put my time-warped head in mind of my high school fraternity lead-outs. After about twenty minutes the road goes through a poaching-control park checkpoint and becomes a one-lane sandy track winding through pine and white-mangrove forest, then opening up to views of lagoons, and swamp and resting flocks of flamingos, bright as hibiscus hedges in the early sun, and ending finally at a small dock, a few geriatric boats, a large thatch-roof, open-air shed where you rig up for the day, and more fishing than you could cover in a lifetime.

Not even with the indefatigable Lazaro—who has been both an angling guide and a ranger in the park since 1995, and who told me he often poles as many as twelve round-trip miles a *day*. On the two days that I fished the flats with him, we never made it more than a couple of miles from the dock, but there was no need to go farther. Most of the flats we fished, wading some and poling others, were hard sand and turtle grass; the rest were marl or a yellowish stone. They ranged in size from an acre or so to twenty times that, and the many bonefish we found on them averaged between three and five pounds, though we caught more than a few bigger than that. Des had shots at permit, too, one day, and there were plenty of barracuda around.

Bonefish country tends to be as uniform as it is easy on the eyes. Unlike trout and salmon rivers, flats and their watery environs all look pretty much alike no matter where you find them. But there was for me a sort of prelapsarian purity about the flats at Las Salinas that distinguished them, and that caused me to often put down my rod for a while to better enjoy it. Lazaro and I had lunch the first day with Ethan and his guide on one of the countless cays that give those flats, immense as they are, a feeling of being broken into discrete keyholes and basins. A disgruntled common black hawk was on its nest in a casuarina thirty feet away from where we sat on the sand and ate.

During the morning we had seen flamingos, ibis, egrets, herons, terns, pelicans, and ospreys—and not a sign that there had been a human anywhere near this coastline since October 27, 1492, when Columbus declared it "the most beautiful land human eyes had ever seen." Ethan lives in Manhattan, about which no one is likely to say that, and to which he had to return the next day. This was, moreover, the first day of bonefishing ever, for that hyper-aware young man, and though it was hardly that for the geezer who lunched with him, the innumerable pleasures of the moment were equally fresh and vivid to both of us.

Because of the distance from the launch site at Las Salinas to the Bocas, you could only get out to them in good weather, and because we had that in spades for our entire stay, Des and I were both able to fish there. Des, at least, will never forget it.

You get to that remarkable fishery via an hour's putter from Las Salinas in an often-patched twelve-foot rowboat powered by a crotchety 9.9-horsepower Yamaha outboard. The approach to the barrier island is around cays, over dozens of flats, and across a wide stretch of deeper water full of bonefish muds. Along its thirty-kilometer length, the island is divided by five channels that run from the open ocean on its south side to the shallow water on its north. Each about a half mile long and sixty- to a hundred-feet wide, these channels and the little creeks and bays that run off of them are 24/7 fish cafeteria lines—unless, that is, there is a strong south wind blowing, as there was on our second day in the Zapata, when Lazaro and I were out there.

Blowing off a turbulent ocean, that wind and an incoming tide reduced both the visibility of the water in the channels and the fish population in them to zero, and for four of the five hours we were there, I might as well have been blind-casting on my lawn. Finally, around 2 p.m. the tide turned and the water began to clear. In the hour before we had to leave to be back at the dock by the park-legislated 4 p.m. deadline, I jumped two tarpon out of small schools and saw maybe a dozen more, along with a big, unhungry snook.

On the boat ride back Lazaro told me about how good the fishing *can* be in the channels and on the island's oceanside flats with a light north wind. And on our last day, Des got to experience exactly that. It was, he said, like fishing in an aquarium packed to the walls with tarpon, snook, jacks, cubera and mutton snapper, grouper, barracuda, sharks, and rays. Well . . . it couldn't have happened to a nicer guy.

All four of our days on the Zapata were trophy angling experiences, but it was the third I would like to hang on my wall if I could find someone to mount it. On that day we boarded the bus with the guides a little earlier than usual for an hour and change drive northwest, at first along the highway to Havana and then over a series of smaller and smaller dirt roads, past palm-thatched huts with pigs rooting in their dirt yards, to the *deep* country fishing concession and military post on the Rio Hatiguanico. Tied to the dock there was a big party boat used for river tours, and five or six roomy, well-kept fifteen-foot jon boats with center consoles and 25-horsepower outboards. The four of us could have each taken one of them and a guide for the day, but I was in the mood for a little camaraderie, so I shared a boat with Richard in the morning and with Des in the afternoon.

From the dock, we followed a small feeder stream for about fifteen minutes to where it joined the main river. The banks were jungly with mangroves and palms. Ospreys and buzzards circled overhead, and kingfishers, herons, and flocks of sanderlings flushed out ahead of us. Buried in a practically unpopulated area of the park, untouched by industry and agriculture and very lightly so by the fishing and river-touring concession, the Hatiguanico is a true wilderness river, and one of the loveliest I have ever been on. When we idled out of the feeder stream into it, the breath hung up in my throat. From that point, the river flows some thirty kilometers westward through virgin forests and swampland to the sea, and before I had even wet a line I had an almost irresistible, if unbalanced, impulse to ditch my plans for the next few days and bribe somebody into floating, fishing, and camping me down the whole thing.

But as at Las Salinas, from a strictly fishing point of view, there is no reason at all on this river to go very far from the dock. The Hatiguanico contains fair to good populations of snook, cuberas, and jacks, but it is primarily, and gloriously, a juvenile tarpon fishery. Though many are caught there between twenty and forty pounds, and a few between sixty and eighty, the tarpon average five to fifteen pounds (by far my favourite size for that fish). And the river quite literally teems with them. After a slow start, from about eleven o'clock on there seemed to be tarpon rolling every-where we looked. Taking half-hour turns, Richard and I cast quick-sink tips into the mangroves along the banks, and to rolling fish in bays where the river widened from its normal sixty or so yards across to over a hundred. I was fishing a weighted Black Death, confected especially for this trip by the great Utah fly tier C. V. Child; and all day long it was the right fly at the right time and place—a situation as sweet as it is rare for me. For a stretch of about three hours in the afternoon with Des, I was putting a tar-pon in the air at about every third cast—including one of close to thirty pounds that was more fish than either I or my eight-weight wanted.

In fishing as otherwise, some days are diamonds and others are stone. In my experience they just about balance each other out—which means I might have a number of rocky salmon days coming this summer to compensate for the Hatiguanico. I am happy to take them.

Richard French is an excellent angler, companion, and trip host. He is also a world-class enjoyer of life, with a somewhat old-fashioned, good cook's knack for creating that enjoyment with

whatever ingredients come to hand, rather than buying them over
the Internet. Just as my father and his friends did at Walker's Cay.
It is Richard's custom on the trips that he hosts to the Zapata to
hold an aprés-fishing cookout on the last day for both the guides
and the sports in the big open-air shed at Las Salinas. Sometimes,
he spit-roasts a whole pig, but whole pigs were in short supply
when we were there, so while he and Des and Eric and I were out
on the flats, Juan Miranda—a good-natured Chilean, who is the
general manager / troubleshooter for Richard's angling operations
in Cuba—cooked up a huge pot of pork shoulder Cuban-style,
with lots of onions and tomatoes. It was served with another big
pot of peeled, boiled potatoes, a tomato-and-onion salad, and a
cooler full of Cristal cerveza. And all that was followed by two
bottles of rum, some of the best cigars on the planet, and a dramatically setting sun.

Lazaro, Gilberto, Eduardo, and Juan Carlos each had their pictures taken with their sport, with each other, and finally with all of
us in a group. Then they ate and drank some more. God knows
they had earned it. At most bonefish destinations these days,
guides make between $400 and $650 a day, and often do as much
running as they do poling. Lazaro and his friends pole for eight
hours every day, and are paid by their government somewhere
around $25 a month—or less than eighty-five cents a day. Not that
they are complaining. Lazaro, who has been at his job for sixteen
years, told me that he couldn't imagine doing anything else, or
working anywhere other than the Zapata Peninsula.

In Miami, New York, Toronto, and many other places, there
are developers and other business opportunists waiting like buzzards on power poles for the cruel and senseless fifty-year-old
American trade embargo against Cuba to lift. Given the way the
world works, it is likely that within the next few decades there will
be a Hyatt on the Hatiguanico and most certainly a "bonefish

destination" at Las Salinas. On the bus ride back to Playa Larga in the dark—after the rum had been drunk, the stogies smoked, the stories told—I just hoped I would have time enough to get my grandsons down to the Zapata when each of them turns ten—to experience it in the same way, and at the same age, as I did.

8

CAPE COD COMEBACK

Back in the good old days of striped bass fishing on Cape Cod, Anton Stezko practically lived in his waders. During the day, whenever he could make himself stay awake, he ran his little offset printing business, the Cape Copy Shop in Orleans. But his real life began every evening when he put on his waders, grabbed his surf rods, and hit the beaches of Nauset or Monomoy for another night of striper fishing. He would fish from just before sunset until just before dawn, timing it so that he could drop off his catch at the fish market and still "beat the birds"—be home in bed before chirping birds could steal any of the three or four hours of sleep he allowed himself before opening up the shop again.

From the moment he moved to the Cape from New Jersey in 1974, Anton dedicated himself to learning the beaches, and it paid off. In those days if a man knew what he was doing he could earn as much as a couple of thousand dollars from a single night of fishing. There was a group of them: Jimmy Costas, Tony Chiarappo, Frank Dagnaut. Everyone was very aggressive, very competitive, and there were lots of big fish to be competitive over. *Cows*. One night Anton caught seven fish over fifty pounds apiece. On another night, he caught thirty-three stripers whose combined weight of fifteen hundred pounds collapsed the springs of his Scout.

And then in early November of 1981, Anton Stezko caught the cow of cows. Fishing near the Pochet Hole on Nauset Beach, using a live eel for bait, he hooked a fish that was so hard to move he figured at first it was foul-hooked. When he finally beached it, he and his friend Jimmy Costas thought it looked more like a seal than a striper. The next day he took the fish to two tackle shops and it weighed seventy-three pounds at both places. It was fifty-five inches long, with a thirty-eight-inch girth: the new twenty-pound-test line-class world-record striped bass. And the last one of over seventy pounds to be caught on the Cape or the outlying islands of Nantucket and Martha's Vineyard since then.

Anton says now that he and his friends thought the party would go on forever—that not even fifteen hundred pounds of striper meat in the back of his truck from one night's fishing caused him to worry that maybe he and everyone else might be taking too many fish, that the resource might be limited and that limit close at hand. But in fact by that November night in 1981, the Atlantic striped bass population had been in trouble for almost a decade and was within two or three years of total collapse. And Anton Stezko's personal revelation, his intimation of the collapse, was closer than that.

Fishing pressure at Nauset had gotten so heavy that he had started fishing the Monomoy beaches. One night he and two friends were coming back from Monomoy near dawn through thick fog in a fourteen-foot skiff with a 25-horsepower engine, running on compass bearings carved into the stern seat of the boat. The skiff was full of dead cow stripers, as usual, and Anton was lying on top of them. Believing they knew where they were, they nearly ran aground on a piece of land none of them had ever laid eyes on before—a lifeless wasteland of a place covered in dead trees. Lying on top of the striper carcasses, Anton seemed to feel the desolation of the place in his soul. It suddenly hit him that the striped bass he had been fishing for since he was a kid were going to be wiped out—their once marvelous population rendered as ruined and empty as this place—and he very nearly wept. Anton determined that night to stop killing so many stripers, but it didn't really matter: In no time at all, there were no stripers around left to kill.

The Atlantic coast commercial harvest of striped bass peaked in 1973 at almost fifteen million pounds. By 1983 that harvest had declined to 3.5 million pounds—a 77 percent decrease caused by overharvesting and habitat degradation in Chesapeake Bay and the Hudson River, the number one and number two spawning grounds for the Atlantic coast stripers. In response, Congress passed the Atlantic Striped Bass Conservation Act in 1984, forcing the states within the Atlantic range of the striped bass from North Carolina to Maine to comply with the provisions of a striped bass management plan drawn up by the Atlantic States Marine Fisheries Commission, or face a complete moratorium on striper fishing within their waters. All of the states complied eventually, and some went quickly beyond compliance. Maryland and Delaware imposed their own commercial and recreational moratoria in their state waters in 1985. New York, Rhode Island, and Connecticut closed their marine waters to striper fishing in 1986, and Virginia followed in 1989. North Carolina closed its ocean waters from 1984 through 1990.

Prompt and laudable as all this action was on the part of state and federal agencies, many people believed that it was too little, too late—that the Atlantic striped bass fishery was essentially beyond recovery. But it wasn't, and the demonstration of that fact is one of the very few great American fishery-conservation success stories.

Massive environmental cleanup efforts in the Hudson and the Chesapeake during the mid to late '80s, severe harvest limitations on both commercial and recreational fishing throughout the Atlantic range of the striper, and effective enforcement of those limitations proved that human beings can sometimes earn a second chance from nature, and, by beginning decisively to do what we should have been doing all along, bring back a species put within spitting distance of extirpation. The recovery took ten years and change, but by 1996 it was a full, glorious, and rewarding one: The value that year of striped bass landings in the commercial fishery of $8 million was the highest since 1975, and recreational angler expenditure on striped bass fishing reached $560 million, a 35 percent annual growth in revenue over the $85 million of 1981. And since 1996 things have only gotten better. In fact, many old-timers from Cape Hatteras to the Kennebec will tell you to forget about the 1960s and '70s—that the real striper good old days are right now.

As someone who had witnessed a little of both the heyday and the crash and burn of striper fishing along the Atlantic coast (and had given up fishing for them entirely in the mid-1980s), I had been curious for some time to see this comeback for myself, and, in particular, to experience on Cape Cod what my friend Tom Rosenbauer, a vice president and catalog manager for the Orvis Company, had been telling me for years was "some of the most unbelievable flats fishing you've ever seen." So not long ago Tom Montgomery and I hied off to the Cape to meet up with Rosenbauer and to try out as many methods of fly rodding for stripers as we could pack into three days.

To steal an image out of an old enthusiasm of mine, Cape Cod looks like nothing so much as the flexed left shoulder and arm of a bodybuilder in the classic double-biceps pose. The shoulder is around Scussett state beach; the hand is Provincetown; the outside of the forearm is Nauset beach; Bass River is at the center of the triceps; and Chatham is the elbow. Falling off that elbow to the south toward Nantucket, like a couple of drops of posing oil, are the Monomoy islands.

Only a mile or so offshore from Outermost Harbor in Chatham, those islands are a national wildlife refuge and an important rest stop and nesting grounds for thousands of terns, piping plover, and other migratory birds. On the western sides of both North and South Monomoy—whose combined length is some seven or eight miles—are hundreds of acres of white sand flats and patches of eelgrass. These flats warm up earlier in spring than the surrounding waters of Nantucket Sound and attract hordes of striped bass on their migratory route north from the Chesapeake and the Hudson. The bass start showing up at Monomoy in late April and are there in force by Father's Day. Though the fishing can be good into October when the stripers begin to migrate south again, the prime months on the flats are June and July when it is not at all unusual, David Steeves told us, to see hundreds, even thousands of fish in a day, or for an angler to have as many as a hundred shots at stripers from the bow of Steeves's eighteen-foot Hewes Bonefisher.

That boat is particularly at home on the Monomoy flats, whose white sand, grass beds and clear water, whose ceruleans and tans and turquoises and creams are so evocative of bonefish flats in the Bahamas and other tropical places that it can be downright disorienting. And as with most bonefish destinations, a poled flats skiff and your own legs provide the most effective methods of fishing the place.

It was cool and partly sunny when David began poling some hundred yards off the west side of the south end of South Monomoy in three to four feet of water. The water temperature was 64 degrees, right about where you want it; the wind was light; the visibility fair but improving. Oystercatchers and terns were in the air everywhere over the island, which was low and dune-like and covered in places with stately spartina.

I took the bow with an eight-weight fly rod, a clear, intermediate sinking line and a long olive-and-white Clouser, tied to resemble a sand eel. Within minutes a couple of bluefish idled by and I caught one of them. The stripers were tougher. We saw lots of them—singles, doubles, and small schools, moving over the flats more purposefully and quickly it seemed than bonefish normally do, but they were spooky and discriminating. I had four or five fish follow the Clouser for a distance then turn off, as others did from Montgomery's fly when he took the bow.

Around eleven the stripers came on the feed and I caught two in ten minutes, both out of schools, both explosive, silver-sided fish of around eight pounds. David told us that these were about average size for the fishery, though a few are caught on the Monomoy flats each season in the twenty-five- to thirty-five-pound range. Massachusetts regulations allow an angler to keep one striper per day, so long as it is twenty-eight inches or over. But neither David nor any of his clients has killed a bass in the four years he has guided at Monomoy. At twenty-seven, Steeves is old enough to remember the mid-1980s, though the crowds of fish we saw and cast to that day could tempt even an old hand into taking their presence for granted.

We fished in water as deep as four or five feet—looking for the black, moving, cloud-like shapes of schools or for the silver flashings of feeding fish—to as shallow as two feet, where individual fish were easy to spot against the white sand. For about four hours Montgomery and I caught stripers out of schools and spotted singles, blind-casting over eelgrass beds and throwing poppers to busting fish. Later in the afternoon they lost their appetites again on a rising tide, and the catching came to a full stop.

After an hour or so of fruitless poling and searching, David Steeves said, "I just had an idea. Would you guys like to go see the seals on the other side of the island?"

"Did David ask you if you wanted to go see the seals?" said Tony Biski the next morning. I was telling him how the fishing had petered out the afternoon before.

"As a matter of fact . . ."

Biski laughed, as he is very prone to do. "That's the code here for 'It's all over, boys. Reel 'em up.'"

Biski moved to the Cape in 1977 from Troy, New York, and became a commercial fisherman who striper fished for fun every chance he got. About ten years ago he started seeing stripers on the flats around Monomoy on his runs out to the commercial fishing grounds and he tried fishing for them with plugs and sand eels but couldn't catch them. Shortly after that, someone (Tony is not sure who) figured out the similarities between what they had at Monomoy to bonefishing and started throwing flies to the stripers, and one of the most unique and interesting saltwater fisheries in North America was born.

Knowing a good thing when he saw it, Tony became a sportfishing guide in 1992, and he and the Benson brothers, Bob and Richie, were the first to start adapting classic flats fishing techniques to Monomoy for clients—the Bensons with poled skiffs, and Tony by taking his sports out to the flats in his old twenty-one-foot boat, the *Take It EZ*, and wading with them after the fish. It soon became clear that wading, in the clear water and on the hard sand bottoms of Monomoy, was at least as effective a way to catch the stripers there as from a flats boat, and often more so, and now Tony and the two or three other guides who specialize in wading have booming businesses.

That fact is just one of many things that delight big Tony—who with his white mustache and startled eyes, his beefy forearms and zippy wit, and endless supply of chatter and one-liners, could be Santa Claus on speed and an extended fishing vacation. If Santa Claus is Italian. "You're gonna *love* this guy," Tom Rosenbauer had told me.

Rosenbauer has been fishing with Tony, sometimes three or four times a season, since 1992, and the two men have an irreverent client/guide relationship. "I don't guide him at all," says Biski. "The guy's like a crazed, caged dog. I just bring him out here and turn him loose."

He has a point. A widely respected fly tier, author, and flyfishing expert, Rosenbauer is also one of the two or three most insatiable, impassioned, and indefatigable anglers I have ever met. On the short ride out of Monomoy from the marina in Harwich Port where Tony keeps his boat, Rosenbauer scanned the water for stripers as if looking for the cure for cancer. "*Nice* fish!" he would yelp occasionally. "Oh Jesus, Tony, what a pig that one was." And Tony barely had the engine killed at our first anchorage of the day before Rosenbauer had scrambled off the stern in his waders and trotted off toward the horizon, whipping the fly line out of his rod. We didn't see him again for hours.

Montgomery and I waded with Tony just as you would wade for bonefish—pausing occasionally to scan the water around us, pushing as little wake as possible—in water that ranged from mid-calf to hip deep, on the outer flats, along the sides of sandbars and up into channels. Doing this when the fishing is on, Tony's clients have some truly banner days—seeing school after school of hundreds of fish each, and catching up to thirty or forty in a day, some of them big. Rosenbauer, for example, released four over thirty-six inches (in the twenty-pound range) one day recently with Tony, plus fifteen or so smaller ones. When the fishing is off, as it was on our two days with Biski, it is still anything but boring. In bad light on the first day and perfect conditions on the second, Rosenbauer, Montgomery, and I saw and cast to lots of fish, including a few hogs, and caught some of them; but on the whole the stripers were moody and unhungry, and far more often than not would follow the fly, heartstoppingly, and then turn off at the last minute. This was true even with various Biski and Rosenbauer crab patterns that they claimed were surefire on picky eaters.

On the day we fished with David Steeves, a Sunday, there had been eight or ten boats working the flats; on Monday and Tuesday with Tony we had those flats—and the black-backed gulls, plovers, and oystercatchers, the clouds of terns, the blindingly white sand and multihued water—practically to ourselves. It was enough to turn one positively poetic.

On Tuesday, after wading all morning, we returned to the boat around noon, considerably hungrier than the fish, and fell on the very good sandwiches that Tony had provided. Rosenbauer wolfed his sandwich down and was back in the water wading again practically before Montgomery and I had the cellophane off of ours.

"There's some peaches in the cooler," said Tony when Montgomery and I had finished our lunch and were lolling with cigars, taking in the beauty of the stainless place and day.

"Do you *dare* to eat a peach?" I asked my man Montgomery, tempting him into a little of the Eliot-quoting that he and I are wont to practice whenever fishing is slow.

"Ahhhh," he said, rising to the bait. "'No! I am not Prince Hamlet, nor was meant to be; /Am an attendant lord, one that will do/To swell a progress, start a scene or two . . .'"

"'I grow old, I grow old . . . ,'" I added. "'I shall wear the bottoms of my trousers rolled.'"

Tony Biski was watching us with a kind of sideling alarm, as if we had simultaneously fallen victim to some horrid little verbal seizure that might possibly grip him next. Could it be the sandwiches? Reassured perhaps after a few seconds of silence, he said, "You guys have some kind of problem with peaches?"

No doubt inspired by the poetry at lunch, Montgomery stalked and caught two stripers that afternoon on a crab fly, one of them the biggest bass of the trip. Then the fish quit eating again and Tony asked us if we wanted to go see the seals.

On Cape Cod in these new glory days you can catch striped bass on the flats, off the jetties, in the estuaries, in offshore rips, and in tidal rivers. You can catch them using flies, plugs, jigs, live eels, sea worms, and squid, on almost any kind of tackle you can think of. And you can still catch them at night on the beaches of Nauset and other places, the way Anton Stezko and his friends used to do in the old glory days. You can even do that—as Tom Rosenbauer,

Montgomery, and I did on our last evening on the Cape—with Anton Stezko himself guiding you.

Anton has been a sportfishing guide since 1982, shortly after his fog-bound experience with the ruined landscape. He guides only fly fishermen, two or three nights a week—though there is enough demand for him to guide every night if he wanted to—and he fishes another three or four nights a week on his own. Anton still practically lives in his waders.

We met him at his copy shop around 6 p.m., and spent a few minutes looking at the wood carvings and lovely watercolors he does in what little spare time he has. Anton is tall, kinky-haired, and animated. In his shop he was a pinwheel of enthusiasm showing us his pictures and carvings, but at this time of day fishing is always at the top of his agenda, and when Montgomery and I started to dawdle over the watercolors, he hurried us out the door and onto the road to Nauset beach.

There we parked his 4x4 out on the sand, put on waders and stripping baskets, and walked for twenty minutes out a long sand spit with open ocean on one side, and a narrow bay and then the mainland on the other. A fat red sun was setting over the Cape. There were skimmers and thousands of terns on the wing. Across the bay, lights were coming on in a huddle of prim, well-fed cedar-shake cottages on a bluff. Using big Clousers and fast-sink-tip lines we stood knee-deep in the bay and cast up and across the incoming tide as though it were a river, using mends and the current to take the flies deep.

The fishing here and on the other beaches Anton frequents, he told me without missing a cast, is just great again, from early May right up to December. He catches his biggest fish in September, though the striper comeback is not yet old enough to produce the sixty and seventy pounders that he and his buddies used to catch. He believes it will produce them soon enough, and in the meantime there are more fish than ever—more even than in the 1970s when it seemed to Anton there were too many ever to run out.

He and I and the two Toms caught lots of these comeback stripers, with the old houses on the bluff staring down at our fishing like a porch full of great-aunts gossiping together in the closing dark about things that come and go. Before walking out around nine thirty to a sky filling with stars, we beached maybe two dozen strong, healthy, six- to twelve-pound bass that might one day be seventy-pound cows, unhooked them all, and watched them swim away.

9

IMPARADISED

The girl carelessly dropt a cloth, which covered her and ap-
peared to the eyes of all beholders as Venus showed herself to
the Egyptian shepherd, having, indeed, the celestial form of
that goddess. The capstan was never hove with more alacrity.
At last our cares succeeded in keeping these bewitched fellows
in order, though it was no less difficult to keep the command of
ourselves.

—Louis de Bougainville

Thus did the captain of the French frigate *Boudeuse* describe his
ship's first encounter with the seductions of Polynesia. It was April
of 1768, and Bougainville had just made the second European
discovery of Tahiti, following by only ten months the English captain Samuel Wallis and the HMS *Dolphin*. Captain Bougainville
was a practical man: a diplomat, classicist, and mathematician,
later in life an admiral, senator, and member of the Legion of
Honor. But in Tahiti, like Wallis and his crew, Bougainville and his
men soon found themselves "imparadised . . . transported," as he
put it, "into the Garden of Eden." Wallis, being English, was made

nervous by that transportation; Bougainville and his men simply enjoyed it with Gallic brio and humor.

After six scurvy-ridden months at sea, the explorers found themselves confronted just beyond the hot beach with fragrant shade and bending trees of breadfruit and coconuts, with well-tended orchards of fruit, and streams cascading from the green hills. The men of the island brought them pigs, fowl, and bundles of fruit, and lined up parades of beautiful girls onshore, inviting the sailors to take their picks. "They pressed us to choose a woman and come onshore with her," wrote Bougainville, "and their gestures, which were not ambiguous, denoted in what manner we should form an acquaintance with her." And those parading girls themselves openly encouraged the sailors with "droll, wanton tricks."

Bougainville named this astonishing place Nouveau Cythera for the Greek island where Venus emerged from the sea, and he and his men stayed imparadised there for a couple of weeks, everywhere finding "hospitality, ease, innocent joy and every appearance of happiness," as well as a refreshingly open and un-European approach to relations between the sexes. As Bougainville's botanist, Dr. Philippe Commercon, rhapsodized: "They know no other god than love. Every day is consecrated to him, the whole island is his temple, all the women are the idols and the men the worshippers. And what women! The rivals of the Georgians in beauty, and the sisters of the unveiled graces. Here, modesty and prudery lose their tyranny. The act of procreation is an act of religion; its people, and its end is greeted by universal applause."

Imparadised indeed: What Wallis and Bougainville were the first Europeans to discover was not so much an island as the ultimate fulfilment of the sea adventurer's oldest dream, as ancient as the fable of the Sirens: a mild place of flawless beauty and ease where the Youth of the World dallied day and night with neither inhibition nor guilt. The discoverers paid for their participation in that dalliance in the coin of nails off their ships and venereal disease. They introduced to the island the Paradise-killing concepts of private property and sin, and opened the way to missionaries who would use those concepts to turn the dallying Youth of the World into workaday middle-agers, just like you and me.

But never mind. Tahiti and her sister islands have continued to sing like Sirens of various fulfillments to adventurers ever since that maiden dropt her cloth on Bougainville's ship, and dreams as long as your leg still beckon there like waving palms from bowers just beyond the hot beaches.

> *What madness possessed me to thrill and yearn over these far-flung spots of the globe, unknown to fishermen? . . . But that is the way I am made! The ideal was to gain them all, a natural, excusable and almost futile ambition.*
>
> —Zane Grey

The dreams Captain Jody Bright has chased for most of his life all have marlin bills on them, and the bigger the bills the better. Jody grew up in Port O'Connor, on the Gulf Coast of Texas, where his father owned a gamefishing boat and was founder and organizer of the Poco Bueno Big Game Fishing Tournament, one of the country's richest and wildest angling competitions. Jody tried to quit high school to go to work on charter boats, but his parents wouldn't let him. He did quit college after one year and went to work as a deckhand in Cozumel, Mexico, where after a while the top-gun Hawaiian charter captain Bobby Brown rode into town on a forty-three-foot Merritt. Jody hired on with Brown as a deckie, and hasn't lived a solid month of mainland life since.

For seven years he bounced around the Caribbean, fishing in Bimini, St. Thomas, Isla Mujeres, Venezuela, and Puerto Rico. In 1985 he got his captain's license, and in 1987 he moved to Hawaii to specialize in the South Pacific and giant blue and black marlin. He has fished over a decade of seasons for the thousand-pound and bigger blacks that congregate each fall on Australia's Great Barrier Reef. He has fished the Society Islands and New Guinea, and made scouting trips to the Solomons, the Tuamotus, and Vanuatu, looking for new congregations of fish in virgin water: frontier fishing, he calls it. And since Cozumel, he has brought to hand over two thousand marlin.

What Jody Bright would most like to find on the frontiers he fishes is a spawning congregation of big female Pacific blue marlin like the spawning congregation of blacks on the Great Barrier Reef. Somewhere in that congregation would likely be Big Mama, his ultimate dream—a blue larger than the 1,376-pound female caught out of Kona, Hawaii, by Bobby Brown's boat on a day Jody was supposed to be Brown's wireman but jumped into another boat to help out a friend; bigger maybe even than the black Jody had on the wire nine times last year on the Reef, a fish that would have smashed Alfred Glassell's 1,560-pound record set in 1953—a fish close to 2,000 pounds that came in straight up and down, instead of suspended, so the entire crew couldn't lift it and had to just stand there at the transom and watch sharks eat it all the way up to the pectoral fins.

For the last few years Jody Bright has been studying long-liner reports and a sixteen-country South Pacific commercial fishery database. Recently, he decided he knew where Big Mama might live, and he asked me to come fish for her with him—on a bank he wouldn't tell me the name of, in something called the Tuamotu Archipelago.

As he was in so many places, the writer Zane Grey was the first sportsman to look for marlin in the Tuamotus, fishing for almost a month there in 1927 on the first of three frontier fishing trips he made to the South Pacific. A sort of 1920's version of Louis L'Amour, Grey was one of two celebrated American novelists to write extensively on big game fishing, the other, of course, being Ernest Hemingway. And while Grey was not the writer Hemingway was, Hemingway was not nearly the angler-adventurer that Grey was. There was not a whiff of posturing in Grey's fishing and adventuring: He did both as simply and intently as a farm boy putting his pole on his shoulder, trudging off to any pond within walking distance, and there fishing passionately and joyfully, not for some new element of persona but for his dream of what lived in the pond.

Grey went to the Tuamotus because of reports he heard in Tahiti of giant yellowish marlin that lived there, marlin so ferocious that they attacked native canoes with bills protruding from their lower, rather than upper, jaws. Though he never found such a fish (nor has anyone else), it was, like Big Mama, a dream worth fishing for—even if that fishing had to be done in the exact middle of nowhere.

Along with the Marquesas Islands just to the north, the Dangerous Archipelago—as Captain Bougainville name the Tuamotus—is farther away from any major landmass than any place on Earth, stretching for almost a thousand miles across the South Pacific between Australia to the west and South America to the east. The archipelago consists of seventy-six atolls, the coral islet-ringed remnants of ancient volcanic craters. Some of those atolls have passes through their reefs, allowing safe access to them, and some do not. About half are inhabited, most only by a handful of people who fish, farm black pearls, and raise copra for a low-stress and pleasant living. Taken as a whole, the atolls, with their lagoons and surrounding waters, make up one of the last great fishing, diving, and sailing adventuring grounds left on Earth.

Rangiroa is the most populous and visited of the Tuamotus, and the largest atoll in the South Pacific. Its 240 *motus* surround the world's second largest lagoon, more than a hundred miles in circumference, entering which for the first time Zane Grey nearly put his yacht, *Fisherman*, permanently onto coral. Our yacht, a forty-seven-foot, totally tricked-out Buddy Davis sportfisherman called the *Horea Royal*, was more fortunate, and was waiting for us, moored just off the dock of Hotel Kia Ora, when we arrived there after a two-hour flight from Bora Bora on the day of the full moon we had come to fish.

There are no first-rate gamefishing boats or crews based in the Tuamotus, so Jody Bright had chartered the *Horea Royal* from her homeport on the Society Island of Tahaa. The boat had made the nineteen-hour crossing in high winds the day before, crewed by its captain, Yves Guilbert, his Polynesian mate, Francis, and an American named David Beaudet, whom Jody had brought over from Kona, Hawaii, to provide us with a wireman up to dealing with Big Mama should we hook her.

Hotel Kia Ora, built by three Frenchmen in 1972, has the particular spicy blend of chicness, simplicity, and adventurous muscularity that flavors many French resorts around the world.

You sleep there in elegantly spare little bungalows, or *fares*, facing a lovely beach on the lagoon. If you are not questing for marlin, you can spend your days at a variety of activities from windsurfing and some of the world's best diving to *petanque* with a rum and tonic. And despite the hotel's remoteness, you can eat there—in a thatch-roofed, open-air dining room—no less than brilliantly. On the day we arrived, Jody, the crew from the boat,

Tom Montgomery, my wife, Patricia, and I, and our friend Jerome Gary lunched on carpaccio of yellowfin tuna, sashimi, and lobster salad. Then we went fishing.

Jody's plan was to fish out of Rangiroa for a few days, then frontier on, as Zane Grey had, to an atoll called Apataki and use that as a base from which to pound the bank we had come here to fish. On a previous exploratory trip, he had learned a little about the water around Rangiroa but caught no marlin, and neither did we that first afternoon. Instead, we became familiar with the boat and its tackle, and we heard Yves Guilbert's favorite fishing story.

Yves was sixty-five years old, a sparrow-like little Frenchman with a jaunty silver mustache and an earring. In 1949 he was working as a storyboard artist on an Orson Welles movie in Morocco. When some of the film was destroyed, he was brought over to Hollywood to re-create the story for a reshoot. There he heard about a big game fishing tournament in Bimini. Yves had fished for billfish in Morocco and decided to sign up for the tournament. But when he arrived in Bimini he learned it was a two-man-team competition. Yves was in the middle of pitching a fit when a big, smiling American walked up, said he spoke French, and offered to be Yves's partner. They placed second in the competition, and then the American invited Yves to Cat Cay to fish for a few days with his personal skipper. They had good fishing in Cat Cay and the American told Yves that he, too, worked in Hollywood once in a while at screenwriting. It wasn't until Yves got back to California that he learned that Ernest Hemingway, his fishing partner, was anyone special.

Jerome Gary—both our designated interpreter and movie business connection, who himself wears so many hats in the entertainment industry that Patricia and I identify him as the Hollywood Hyphenate—translated this story for the rest of us. At the end of it, Yves shook his dapper little head, gazed back into that old

memory for a moment, and added something. "He says Heming-way spoke elegant, almost dainty French," said Jerome, "but he was a bully with fish."

Once I fished for Atlantic blue marlin in Jamaica with a count who carried a 9 mm Browning pistol everywhere he went and gave famous conch soup lunches. This count would pour brandy into the sea and chant incantations to the fish gods to deliver us a marlin, but not until we were ready. On that first afternoon aboard *Horea Royal* we rigged tackle, tested drags, and felt out ways into the intermeshing of our various positions in the team adventure that is big game fishing.

Jody was the fishing captain: He ran the boat while Yves sat next to him on the flying bridge with a yachting cap on, scanning the waves once in a while with a pair of binoculars. Yves and his mate Francis, whose job on this charter was only to keep the boat clean and orderly, were there because Tahitian law required them to be. David Beaudet, the captain of his own charter boat back in Kona, was our wireman. In marlin fishing you are allowed up to thirty feet of wire or heavy monofilament leader, which is con-nected to your line at one end by a swivel and to your bait or lure at the other end. You fight a fish up to the boat with a rod only so far as the swivel, and it is then the wireman's dicey job to bring the fish the rest of the way in for capture or release by wrapping one hand after another around the leader and hauling the fish in to the transom. Adventure is an effort to bring something only imagined to hand, then someone has to handle it; in our case it was David Beaudet. Tom Montgomery was aboard to take pictures. I was there to fish, Patricia for the ride, and Jerome claimed to be along mostly to charm the locals.

Big game fishing can accurately be described as Napoleon did war: 90 percent immense boredom and 10 percent intense excite-ment. The 10 percent time can be very exciting indeed when big fish are involved, and it needs instinctive, adrenaline-overriding teamwork between crew and angler. The bigger the fish, the more that teamwork is needed. The angler hooks and fights the fish, adjusting the drag and his own labor to react to whatever the fish does, to keep it off balance and turn its head as often as possible. The captain anticipates his angler and uses the boat and sea conditions to help him; the wireman keeps the fighting chair facing the fish, advises the angler on drag or reel-gearing the way a caddy advises a golfer on clubs, and then wires the fish once the angler and captain have positioned it. Fish, even big fish, can be caught without this teamwork (in fact, some captains will tell you they can catch marlin with a corpse in the chair if the corpse can reel), but the beauty and thrill of the sport resides in it—in a seamless synergy of effort once a fish is hooked. When that synergy is going, you're big game fishing; when it's not, you're just ripping lips and putting your health at risk while you're at it.

Jim Everett, with the swivel at the tip of the rod on the fish of his life, a black marlin over a thousand pounds that he has spent more than $200,000 over the years to catch, unhooks from the harness over his captain's screaming objections and lunges for the transom to see this dream, this joy, just as the marlin jumps on the wire; and Jim does see it for a second before the marlin's bill enters his left eye socket and cracks out the back of his skull. Tom Dunphy pushes his drag over the button on a giant bluefin tuna while the boat is backing down, and when the tuna surges, Tom is lifted by the harness overboard and chopped into chum by the props. A Hawaiian angler is pulled overboard by a blue marlin and towed eighty feet underwater before he can free himself.

While trying to release marlin, wiremen have themselves been hooked on the trailing hook of a lure and carried off. David Beaudet has been gored by a bill in the chest and had his left hand broken by a fish. Gaff points, like bills, can skewer you. A 130-

pound test line can lop off fingers, even hands. The gold anodized aluminum reels that hold that line are like small oil drums, and the bent-butt rods they fit onto are thick as ferry hawsers. The tackle and equipment used to catch big marlin is big, and built to inflict big pain and exhaustion. It can hand you your ass in any number of ways, as can the fish themselves, if you don't know what you're doing or try to do it by yourself. For one last cautionary example of faulty teamwork in the pursuit of large creatures that swim, think of Ahab.

By the next day when the fish gods delivered fish, our team was ready. Mostly. At 9:45, the Hollywood Hyphenate did back the drag off into a desperate snarl of line on what might have been a very big marlin, and a hot little two hundred pounder threw the hook on me after jumping all over the ocean for five minutes. But Jerome and I caught six big yellowfin tuna that morning and lost a few more. We could have caught as many yellowfin as we wanted out of the huge schools of them we found crashing bait while hundreds of boobies hovered overhead and dove into the baitfish, but we were just fishing the corners of the schools looking for marlin.

And at one thirty that afternoon, while trolling one of those corners with four lures out, two from flatlines and two from outriggers, a big marlin bill came up behind the left 'rigger. The fish swirled at the lure and missed it, then charged the lure on the left flatline, swirled again, and disappeared. "Try reeling in fast about twenty yards," said David Beaudet. Leaving the flatline rod in its holder on the transom, I reeled in twenty yards of line, making the lure skip, then let it troll again and the fish immediately ate it in a giant boil of water. I carried the rod into the chair, fixed the butt into the gimbal, clipped the kidney harness into the reel, and watched the line pour off against forty pounds of drag. When the fish's first run was over, I leaned into the harness, pumping the rod and looking through muscle memory for the exact timing of exerted effort that makes for the right combination of force and smoothness. The fish jumped twice, showing weight carried all the way back to its tail, then settled down and fought deep.

We were only about five hundred yards off the reef of Rangiroa and I could watch palm trees bouncing to the trade winds. The day was perfect. Boobies dove into a bait school a hundred yards off the stern. David swung the chair for me, Jody handled the boat, and I gloried in the paced, sweaty, totally absorbing joy of pitting strength against strength. "I did not think. I only felt," wrote Zane Grey about that joy, which is the beating heart of big game fishing. "How blue the sky, wonderful the water, gorgeous the islands!"

In a little less than forty-five minutes the swivel was at the rod tip and it was David Beaudet's turn to work. David weighs well over two hundred solid pounds, a bigger-than-normal part of which is in his hands, wrists, and forearms. Wiring is done with those body parts, with bent arms and legs, and with total concentration. Once he has the leader, a good wireman never takes his eye off the fish, never straightens his arms or legs, and never goes tentative. Wiring is a lot about finesse (David says it feels like flying a giant kite), but it is even more about straight-ahead, often violent determination. Tom Montgomery—a Wyoming-based trout fishing guide whose clients and associates customarily handle fish as if they were infants before releasing them—had never seen big game fishing before, and the wiring frenzies of grabbing, wrapping, and wrenching, of flying leader and erupting water, of David clubbing the yellowfin, gaffing them and slinging the huge, blood-gushing, walleyed, tail-thumping fish onto the deck, both horrified and fascinated him. Now, trying to photograph the big marlin being wired, Tom pried a little too far into David's force field of concentration and got smacked right back out of it again. After that, he kept his distance from David Beaudet's wiring, which on that marlin was brief and efficient. With three hand wraps, David got the fish up on plane—with its thick black bill, its great wild blue eye, its mottled copper and silver gill cover, its indigo shoulder and pectoral fin all riding out of the water—long enough for Jody to punch a tag into the fish's back. Then David snipped the leader at the lure and the fish floated for a moment on the surface, then flicked its tail and was gone.

It was not Big Mama, not even by half, but it was a marvelous fish—somewhere north of seven hundred pounds. It was one of the first and certainly the largest marlin ever caught in the Tuamotus. (Zane Grey hooked, but did not catch, a marlin there, and only three or four sportfishing boats have fished the atolls since then.) It and the other blues we caught and lost there, a total of six, along with the nine or ten yellowfin we caught and as many wahoo bites—all in less than twelve hours of serious trolling— proved this part of Jody's frontier fishery.

But more important for me, that fish was the answer to one of my own dreams. For forty years I have paid my dues to marlin fishing, dragging baits for them in Florida and all over the Caribbean, in Nantucket and North Carolina, in Mexico, Venezuela, Costa Rica, New Zealand, Africa, and Australia. I have gone to bed on literally hundreds of nights and watched bait trails burned into the backs of my eyelids by sun and concentration. And I have caught dozens of marlin. But never, before this one, a Pacific blue, and never any marlin over five hundred pounds. That fish may not have been the dream Jody Bright was after in the Tuamotus, but it was one I had been trying to catch for a very long time. And we still had plenty of time to fish Jody's secret bank and find Big Mama.

That was the thinking anyway, so we took the next day off from marlin fishing to do some surfcasting from the boat into the reef for giant trevally and jacks, and in the afternoon, to take an under-water float through a unique marine menagerie.

Rangiroa offers a smorgasbord of great diving possibilities in improbably clear water, but its most thrilling dive is a forty-five-minute drift on the incoming tide through one of the atoll's two major passes connecting open ocean to the lagoon—a drift that is widely regarded as the finest shark dive in the world. Three hundred yards wide and over a hundred feet deep, Tiputa Pass on the incoming tide is a giant cafeteria line of fish coming into the lagoon to feed. There are brilliant little reef fish, the colors of children's dreams, picking at the coral with their parrot-like beaks and reminding you, maybe, of all the bright and happy things your life is full of; the tame, green hundred-pound Napoleon wrasses; the nervous schools of jacks, barracuda, and ballyhoo; the leopard and manta rays, turtles and dog-toothed tuna. And, quite unforgettably, there are sharks—hundreds of them, mostly three- to five-foot gray reef sharks, a few blacktips, and an occasional fifteen-foot hammerhead—with their remote eyes and prehistoric gill vents and beautiful sleekness, reminding you, maybe, of all the mindlessly threatening things your life is full of. Backed into a coral cave at a hundred feet, your entire view is of sharks overlaid on other sharks; and suspended at sixty feet, drifting upright in the four- or five-knot current, you are surrounded as densely by them as one of those little figures is by "snowflakes" in the plastic balls you shake.

In other places all three of those species of shark have been known to attack people. They don't do that here for some reason, or haven't yet. But one of the many stimulants of the Tiputa Pass dive is imagining how quickly your South Seas adventuring would end if just the sharks within arm's reach were simultaneously to decide to dine before reaching the lagoon on whatever was nearest at fin.

Three days later we finally steamed over to Jody's bank from Apataki. We had made the ninety-mile crossing from Rangiroa to Apataki two days before, catching a marlin almost accidentally on the way, and we had fished for wahoo and picnicked with Jody's friend Jean Tapu and his family on the day after that. Now we had three full days to fish hard for Big Mama in the single place Jody figured her most likely to live—a place he had imagined fishing and kept to himself for seven years, ever since he dug it out of long-liner reports.

It was a flawless marlin day, with a hot, humid, big-fish wind out of the north and just the right chop on the sea. Jody watched Nameless Bank come up on his color video depth recorder, right where it was supposed to be. There were birds working everywhere along the bank. David Beaudet dropped the lures overboard, into that water that no one had ever fished before, water where a marlin too big even to imagine might live . . . and five minutes later the boat broke. A tiny, dream-defeating little thing called an injector seized in the starboard engine of that high-tech half-million-dollar game boat, and suddenly we might as well have been in a canoe.

If the problem had been bad fuel from the barrels Jody had shipped to Apataki, as he and David first believed it was—fuel that was also going to the other engine—we might still be out there, waiting on some *motu* for one of the tankers that pass that way once or twice a year, as there was no Coast Guard, or anyone else for that matter, to call for help. Knowing that, and believing the fuel was bad, Jody dove overboard to lock the prop on the starboard engine, cleaned the fuel filter on the other engine three or four times, and nursed the boat to Apataki at six knots without once looking back at the bank.

"My epitaph will read: 'He came close,'" he said on the way in. Then he added, with a sigh: "Pioneers always get the arrows."

Within sight of Apataki I suggested we put out a lure. We did that and I caught a marlin on it, a feisty little male that grey-hounded us all over the place, endearing itself to me. David wired the fish and snubbed it up to the stern so that Tom could take its picture.

"Let's kill him," Jody said.

"Let's don't," I said.

"The fish are here, the moon is right—this could've been a seven-fish day, a *ten*-fish day with one or two granders. I *really want* to kill this little fucker," said Captain Bright.

But he leaned over the transom, took the hook out of the fish's mouth and let him swim away—dispossessing himself, for the time being anyway, of his madness to thrill and yearn over one far-flung spot of the globe.

As the waves rose, fish appeared in the crystal water, shining, floating, rising, even swimming; and of all the aquarian specta-cles of beauty and life that I had seen this was supreme.

—Zane Grey

Grey was staying on the atoll of Apataki when on a walk along the reef he saw whole schools of fish riding in the sunlit waves—black angelfish in one, tiny fish-like "opal sparks" in another, dark-blue oval fish in another—each school in its own, glittering, cresting aquarium. The sight caused him to go sit beneath a coconut tree and marvel over the magical delights this world offers to anyone who will adventure for them and "watch with wide, slow eyes."

Apataki is still full of magical delights, we learned as we waited there, unable to big-game fish, for a diesel mechanic to fly in from Tahiti. It was another way of learning that dreams are the mothers of adventure.

There are no tourist facilities on Apataki. We stayed in a little bungalow that Jean Tapu uses to house Japanese and American buyers for his black pearls. The bungalow had a concrete deck built out over the lagoon, a couple of feet above the water. At low tide only a few inches of water covered the living coral groves of toadstools, cabbage heads, and fairy shelves, water so transparent that unless a breeze disturbed it, nothing proved there was water there at all. At high tide we could sit in chairs on the edge of the deck and throw bread to parrot fish, needlefish, a four-foot eel, and a little blacktip shark who frisked around like a puppy.

It was a ten-minute walk from the bungalow to Jean's house where we took our meals, or to the broken *Horea Royal* tied up at the municipal dock. If you took that walk in the early morning, with the cool air on your skin like a lotion, there would be a few men working their boats, children sleeping on cots on the covered decks of houses, egrets fishing in the shallows, a spray of ballyhoo being chased by a jack in the lagoon, and roosters crowing and scratching in the coral. If you took it at noon, it would be under a vertical sun that made the dirt streets almost too hot to walk on in bare feet, that put the dogs and chickens and pigs under porches and the people in their houses, leaving outside only laundry hanging limply from clotheslines, and the boats—skiffs, outrigger canoes, the sleepy mahimahi chasers with their tiny bow cockpits, deep-V fishing boats, old flat-bottom-do-it-alls; boats drawn up onto platforms in the lagoon, pulled up onto palm logs on the beach, turned over in yards, and tied to rickety docks; boats in all the vivid colors of the tropics, many of them a sunset orange with yellow, red, and blue piping. And walking the road in the evening, there would be a burnished glow to everything, crabs scurrying into holes for the night, boats out handlining for dogtooth tuna beyond the surf break, and Polynesian music coming from a bun-

galow with one light on and a backlit big-eyed child in undies on
the porch, watching you.

A hundred fifty people live in Apataki, most of them in concrete bungalows with louvered windows, open corridors for wind
to move through, and a pile of coconuts in the yard. Those houses
are painted in the same colors as the boats—the colors of the sky,
the sea, the coconut palms, the coral, the beach. On the shady
main street is the small general store, a post office, the shed for
the generator that powers the island, a school, and a pretty church
with vaulted ceiling beams painted ocean blue. Everywhere you
walk, at any time of day, people smile and say hello, stop whatever
they are doing to talk if you seem to want to, and give you things—
from coconuts to shell necklaces. Old men serenade you with gui-
tars, and children make a gift of dancing spontaneously for you, or
showing off their dives from the town dock.

Some people work on Apataki—at fishing, farming pearls, or
raising copra, mostly; some don't. If you need something and don't
have it, someone will give it to you. Crime on the island is unknown, and so is bureaucracy. Apataki has a mayor, but Jean Tapu
told me they always elect someone stupid to that position so he
will try to please everyone. In all, the island is well characterized
by Louis de Bougainville's 225-year-old description of Tahiti, as a
place of "hospitality, ease, innocent joy and every appearance of
happiness."

Jean Tapu is the biggest employer in Apataki and its leading
citizen. He is also a man who so serenely and naturally combines
the dignity of strength with the humility of gentleness that he
makes that pearl-rare combination in a man seem almost familiar.
In 1967, at thirty-nine years old, Jean went to Cuba to compete in
the annual World Spearfishing Championship, and won it with a
score that is still the highest ever recorded in the competition.

Then, he could free dive to almost 150 feet. Now, at age sixty-four, he still dives regularly to seventy-five feet, and he dives every day.

Jean was one of the first three black-pearl farmers in French Polynesia, and he is now one of the biggest and most successful. This year he has eighty thousand oysters ready for grafting, which means he will harvest fifteen thousand to twenty thousand pearls. He is also, this year, making the first open-water attempt anywhere in the world to raise mahimahi, or dolphinfish, commercially. He and his wife, Estelle, have three grown children and six grandchildren. Two of those grandchildren, teenage boys named Tyrone and Moana, live with him, as does Moana's beautiful girlfriend, Hina. In the mornings, Jean, Moana, and Tyrone step off the deck of Jean's overwater house into a boat and go farm mahimahi or oysters, like firing up the tractor to go to work in the back forty. And when they get tired of working, they go diving or fishing or spearfishing.

While we were on Apataki, we trolled along the outside of the reef with Jean and his family for wahoo, catching as many of those delicious, lantern-jawed sea arrows as we wanted within a hundred yards of the atoll. We free dived with Jean and Tyrone on their pearl farm and watched them bring the nets holding the seeded oysters up from the blue depths of the lagoon, working for sixty to ninety seconds at a time between breaths. Jean brought a few of those oysters home with him to open. They were ten years old, as big around as salad plates, and one of them held a hypnotizingly beautiful, dove-gray black pearl that Jean gave to Patricia as casually as if it were a shell he had picked up on the beach.

And late one afternoon, with the sun a tall man's height off the sea, Jody and I went spearfishing with Tyrone. Finning down fifty or sixty feet, he would lie motionless on the bottom for up to two minutes waiting for a fish to swim by—holding a coral head with his gloved left hand and the long wooden speargun in his right—

before surfacing for another breath. He shot a tubby blue and orange parrotfish, missed a dogtooth tuna, and shot a rainbow runner out of a school of fifty or sixty—hunting as easily as I used to hunt squirrels in my backyard. But there were no sharks in my backyard. When a six-foot blacktip moved in, drawn by the thrashing of the speared rainbow runner, Tyrone hugged the fish to his chest and stabbed it in the head with his knife to kill it quickly, and the shark drifted away.

We stayed in the water until after the sun went down, until almost dark, and the deck of the Tapu skiff was covered with fish when Tyrone finally vaulted over the gunwale into the boat with a big grin, calling it another day of subsistence living.

A phrase from the poet Rimbaud—"The key to the feast of yesterday"—kept occurring to me in Apataki. It felt to me that the island was somehow exactly such a key, and the picnic the Tapus held for us the last day we were there dropped the cloth for me on a vision of what that feast may have been like.

We fished for wahoo in the morning in Jean's boat, trolling down to the north end of the atoll. We had left the Hollywood Hyphenate honeymooning on the beach at Rangiroa, so there were six in our group and five in the Tapus'—plus Pizzalo, their black-and-white, bow-riding, pig-chasing, rolled-tail dog—filling the boat. The trade wind pushed a few fat, bright clouds across a royal-blue sky. The white-beached, green-palmed motus slipped by, breakers flashing on the coral reefs between them. Just after noon we entered the lagoon through a narrow pass and went ashore onto a small, thickly palmed island.

Pizzalo fished for bait with his paws in the gold-green water on the beach; Jody, Patricia, and I surf cast into the purplish-blue water of the pass; and in the emerald water of the lagoon, Jean, Tyrone, and Moana spearfished for lunch. Yves sat on the beach with a cold, but smiling and happy. Always-smiling Francis sat with him. And David Beaudet, with nothing to wire, uncoiled there.

Behind them in a little clearing, Estelle and Hina, with wreaths of flowers in their hair, built a fire and put stones in it to heat. They knocked coconuts out of a tree, poured the milk into a bowl, and grated the meat into another bowl. Estelle mixed some of the coconut milk and meat with farina, made a batter of it, and shaped the batter into pancakes which she cooked between pandanus leaves on the hot stones. She also cooked the speared fish there by laying them whole and ungutted on the stones, and when their bellies burst she and Hina picked the meat off the bones and mixed it with chopped onion, coconut milk, and lime juice. We ate that out of coconut shells with the sweet pancakes of Apataki bread, then we had more Apataki bread crumbled up in coconut milk for dessert.

After lunch, Jean walked the coral beach on the ocean side of the island and brought back to Patricia a handful of perfect shells. And Estelle gave each of us a necklace of shells strung with bright pieces of coral.

While we were packing up to leave the island, four wild sows came out of the palm jungle to root around in the coconut leavings; and as we were wading out to the boat, a four- or five-hundred-pound boar with long, gleaming tusks wandered out to join them. Evidently interested in our group, the boar trotted down to the beach, took a long, nearsighted look at the eleven people in the water staring back at him and collapsed in the sand with a satisfied grunt.

Knowing an imparadised hog when I saw one, I walked back to the beach and scratched his ears.

10

HALDOR'S BITE

In 1936 an Icelandic schoolmaster named Haldor hooked a huge Atlantic salmon in the Grimsa River. After an epic battle, Haldor had just managed to steer the fish into shallow water when the hook pulled out of its mouth. The schoolmaster dropped his rod, threw his considerable person onto the salmon, and thrashed around in the water trying to grasp it. The hard, bright body of an Atlantic salmon being slicker than snot on a doorknob, Haldor was unable to do this. So, with his trophy about to escape, he clamped down on its tail with his teeth and dragged it onto the bank—thus exemplifying for the ages the passion, commitment, and questionable intelligence common to Atlantic-salmon fishermen.

What manner of fish, you wonder, could be worth Haldor's dental bill? Well, it is a marvelous-looking silver bullet of a thing, ranging in size between five and fifty pounds, that when hooked can become a whizzing, leaping frenzy of self-preservation capable of summoning coronaries. Prized for this vivid disinclination to be caught above all gamefish by many of the fanatical anglers who pursue them, Atlantic salmon return each spring and summer from the sea to the precise rivers of their birth in North America and Europe. For sportsmen seeking to catch them on a fly rod, the most productive of those rivers are in eastern Canada, Scotland, Norway, Russia, and Iceland, and in no place are there more of them than in Iceland.

Roughly the size of Kentucky, that astonishingly beautiful little island nation has over one hundred rivers to which salmon return annually, and each of fourteen of those gives up more than eight hundred rod-caught salmon yearly over a ninety-day season. In Iceland the fishing rights to salmon rivers are owned by cooperatives of local landowners who lease out those rights to individuals, groups, or companies who then sell them as rod-days of fishing to roughly fifteen hundred Icelandic anglers and the same number of foreign ones each year. On the top rivers in prime time (July and August on most), a day of fishing—not counting accommodations, food, or guide—will run you between $1,000 and $4,000 per rod, which puts it among the priciest salmon fishing on earth. It is also some of the best, but up until recently that distinction was about the equivalent to being the world's best passenger pigeon shooting.

Over the last forty to fifty years, habitat destruction, pollution, dams, and, primarily, commercial fishing, have depleted the worldwide population of wild Atlantic salmon by two-thirds. That precipitous decline would likely have led to the fish's extinction were it not for the Herculean labors of two relentless and capable salmon preservation organizations, the American-Canadian Atlantic Salmon Federation, and the Iceland-based North Atlantic Salmon Fund. Well-funded primarily by devoted and deep-pocketed salmon anglers, these two organizations have, since the 1990s, bought out most of the commercial salmon nets throughout the North Atlantic, in both the rivers and the open ocean salmon wintering grounds off of Greenland and the Faroe Islands. This strategy of paying commercial fisherman not to fish has been so effective that for almost a decade now the salmon rivers of Iceland

and some of the other North Atlantic countries have entertained record-breaking runs of fish.

The credit for this remarkable turnaround—certainly one of the most singular victories in the history of fishery conservation—belongs to both preservation organizations and dozens of individuals, but to no one more than a troll-like Icelander of terrier tenacity and combativeness named Orri Vigfusson, who founded the North Atlantic Salmon Fund in 1989. Holder of a business degree from the London School of Economics, knighted by the Queen of Denmark, owner of a premier vodka company, Vigfusson has been a tireless hellion of a salmon saver for almost two decades. Raising millions of dollars and preserving millions of salmon by pushing through buyout compliances in Greenland, Ireland, Wales, and Norway, he has, like a modern Haldor, dragged the fish away from loss in his square Viking jaws. In his home country and throughout Europe, Orri is regarded as Mr. Atlantic Salmon, and when he invited Tom Montgomery and me to add two of his pet rivers to a fishing itinerary we were planning to Iceland recently—turning that itinerary into a sort of moveable feast around the country—we leaped like grilse at the opportunity.

The diverse pleasures of a fishing trip to Iceland begin in Reykjavik—a merry, lovable little city which is home to some of the best cuisine and most beautiful women in Europe—and no visiting angler should leave the country without spending at least a couple of days and nights there. It should be mentioned, however, that if you are given to partying, so is Reykjavik, and in the twenty-four hours of daylight it enjoys during the summer, those days and nights can tend to run together into a sleep-deprived, overserved blur not ideally suited to set you up for the rigors of salmon fishing.

In Iceland those rigors include twelve-hour days on the river, from 7 a.m. to 1 p.m. and from 4 p.m. to 10 p.m.; and (as is the case everywhere Atlantic salmon are fished for) they can, and often do, include thousands of fruitless casts, many of them made in weather that can make the whole exercise seem like walking over greased bowling balls waist-deep in freezing water and deluged from above by more of it while throwing baseballs against a howling wind to a nonexistent batter. Then, too, in the regularly exasperating calculus of salmon angling, the weather can be too perfect for good fishing, which is exactly how Tom and I found it on the Fljotaa River, the first course of our moveable feast.

The salmon rivers in Iceland (there are excellent trout and Arctic char rivers there as well) are widely varied both in character and distribution around the country. There are many fine rivers within an hour's drive of Reykjavik, but another of the nonangling pleasures of a fishing trip to Iceland is the stunning drive up the west coast to the northern rivers. Granted, that drive can be har-

rowing, on narrow, often precipitous and foggy roads without guardrails, but it takes you into the very Viking soul of Iceland—around Wagnerian fjords and rugged, windswept headlands, through lava deserts, treeless tan and olive valleys, and lush meadows full of grazing sheep and the stubby Icelandic horses that are both ridden and eaten with relish here. After six hours of such exhilarating driving, Tom and I arrived at Bergland, a small lodge in a meadow above the Fljotaa on one of the country's northernmost capes.

Leased annually by Orri for the use of family and friends, the little river skips down a pretty valley for four or five kilometers between a dam and the sea, and is divided into four one-rod beats. A favorite of Orri's friend Jack Nicklaus, it offers some of the best char fishing in Iceland, as well as a good run of salmon for its size, often yielding five or more salmon a day per person during its prime weeks of late July and early August. We arrived during those weeks but also during a month-long hot and dry period that had the salmon in the river sulky and uncooperative.

On our first evening, the next day, and the following morning, Tom and I were guided by Arni Jorgensen, a newspaper editor and childhood friend of Orri's who had grown up on the river and was as proudly fond of it as if it were a daughter. There were two other anglers at Bergland, and between them, Arni, Tom, and myself, we caught lots of fat, exquisitely colored char and eight to ten salmon in our time there, including a twenty pounder released by Arni on the last morning. But those numbers don't do justice to the experience: wading in shorts and casting small flies on a five-weight trout rod into the sparkling runs of the petite and perky Fljotaa was like having a date with Tammy.

The Laxa i Adaldal, or Big Laxa, is a bit more like Uma Thurman—big, busty, and languidly gorgeous with a dramatic mouth. Near that mouth—with its twin waterfalls plunging into a broad estuarial pool that is one of the most majestic anywhere—is the Big Laxa Angling Club. There we met up with Orri, the club's chairman, on the evening of our third day of fishing, after another spectacular drive west across the top of the country. The club, composed of one hundred international members, is housed in a comfortable lodge that cossets twelve anglers and provides them with some ten miles of the Big Laxa, divided into seven beats. It is a world of fishing, on luscious water, in a verdant, mountain-surrounded valley; and normally it accounts for some of the highest annual catches and largest salmon in the country, regularly yielding twenty to thirty fish a year over twenty pounds and a few over thirty. But like the Fljotaa, the Big Laxa was in a no-rain, warm-water slump, and we and the group of Brits, Spaniards, Icelanders, two Swedes, and a Finn with whom we shared the lodge averaged only about a salmon a day per rod in the day and two half days we were there.

The one of mine I won't forget, a bright, acrobatic henfish of about fifteen pounds, was caught while sharing a rod with Orri on his favorite of all salmon pools—a wide, muscular glide above the waterfalls. After the fish was netted and released, I sat with a stogie on the bank in the nightlong Icelandic twilight and watched Mr. Atlantic Salmon work the pool with his double-handed rod, lost to the world in the sweet physics of casting for the enigmatic creature to which he has devoted most of a lifetime.

Orri is not the first or only person to live out an obsessive zeal for that creature. Century in and century out, no fish has owned so passionate a coterie of devotees, or generated so much ink. Yet despite that long history of intense interest and scrutiny, Atlantic salmon remain essentially, often maddeningly, mysterious. Among a raft of things unknown about them is why you can catch them at all on a fly rod, because when they are in their spawning rivers where they are fly-fished for, they do not feed. And because they don't take your fly out of hunger (as more accommodating fish such as trout do), all questions pertaining to *which* fly they will eat at any given time can be as well answered by a cocker spaniel as any expert. All of which makes the catching of them an inexact science at best, and the great majority of Atlantic salmon fisher-men—including some like myself who have been at it for decades—might admit if waterboarded that the essence of their technique is chuck and chance, and that the good days they have are of as mysterious a provenance as the bad.

But then there are a very few blessed anglers like my friend Peter Rippin, to whom Atlantic salmon fishing is not a science at all but an art bordering on sorcery. These few simply do not have bad days. If the fish are in the river, they catch them, with an eerie combination of skill, Haldorian perseverance, and invention, and what would seem to be some mutant salmon gene in their make-ups that gives them a deep, unfathomable empathy with the fish.

A bright and charming young Englishman, Peter is a partner with two Icelanders in a company called Flyfish Iceland that ar-ranges customized fishing trips for visiting anglers to some of the best salmon rivers and lodges in the country. After a long drive south again we met up with him at one of those lodges on the Nordura River, an hour north of Reykjavik. One of the prettiest and most productive rivers in Iceland, the Nordura was on its way to an all-time record season, with over two thousand salmon al-ready caught from its fifty-five-kilometers of fishable water. On our first evening there, which I unwisely sat out, Peter added five salmon to that total and lost five more. And over the next day and a half he caught an additional seven in difficult, low-water condi-tions, putting on for Tom and me a clinic in getting recalcitrant salmon to bite by dead-drifting small wet flies, tied to long, fine leaders, right into their mouths. It was inspired, coruscating fishing, performed with such utter concentration that Peter's face would fall into a trancelike slackness while he was at it. And it was a pleasure to watch, if—for me, anyway—impossible to duplicate.

The last seat at our moveable feast was down the road a half hour from the Nordura, at the groaning board of the regal and historic Grimsa River, which was also enjoying a record season. Traveling anglers have enjoyed the more than seventy named pools on the Grimsa since the 1870s, when British sports would travel to it by ship and horseback to tent-camp for months on its banks. Those sports were guided by the great-grandfather of Siggi Fjeldsted, the present general manager of the lodge on the Grimsa, and our guide while we were there.

Siggi is a hearty sixty-seven. He started guiding in the mid-1950s at a previous lodge on the river that was built by his great-grandfather in 1901, and run by both his grandfather and father before being replaced by the present lodge in 1971. A fourth-generation Grimsa guide, he knows a thing or two about the river and its salmon, and is more than delighted to tell you about them in a nonstop series of stories that, like the Icelandic Sagas, are full of women and booze and parties, of pratfalls and triumphs and practical jokes, of fish and horses and the celebrities, wimps, and stalwarts he has guided over the decades. They are old-school stories that assume a listener as wry and unhurried, as well-scarred by the pleasures and attritions of maleness, and as contentedly fallen from grace as the bald, bearish, bashed-nose teller. If you are a forty-year-old hedge fund manager with a Blackberry addiction, Siggi might not be your cup of tea. But he was exactly mine, as was everything else about the Grimsa.

The lodge there, designed by the late architect, angling writer, and bon vivant Ernie Schwiebert, is one of the handsomest and most agreeable fishing lodges I know of, with spacious bedrooms, a bright, high-ceilinged living and dining area whose tall windows afford dramatic views of the river, and a superb kitchen. It accommodates only eight rods with the same generous and easy elegance with which the river fishes them, and the overall effect of the place is highly addictive. The convivial group of Icelandic couples with whom we shared the lodge had been coming there in the same week for fifteen years.

But despite loving the place, after eight straight twelve-hour days of moveable feasting, I arrived at the Grimsa wanting badly to push back from the table, and I remained that way. Not even a feisty ten-pound salmon that jumped all over a stripped Sunray Shadow in Ernie Schwiebert's favorite pool on our first evening could pull me out of my mojoless torpor; and while Peter continued to hoodwink fish after fish, I found myself—on this peerless river!—actually looking forward to the monster-Jeeping out of Reykjavik that we had scheduled for our last day in the country.

Evidently having seen this kind of unseemly fade before, Siggi knew exactly how it needed bucking up. At lunch on our second day, with only an evening and a morning of fishing left, he told me he wanted to show me something. After a thirty-minute drive in his old truck, we pulled up in front of his ancestral house, home to four generations of Icelandic salmon addicts. In its living room, hanging on the wall above a sofa, was a life-size wooden carving of a thirty-pound-plus Atlantic salmon—a detailed and truly jaw-dropping representation of none other than Haldor's fish, though the bite marks were missing.

After Siggi had related to me the story of its capture, I felt that I had been slapped on the sidelines by Bear Bryant and told in a shower of spit: "This is Atlantic Salmon Fishing in Iceland, boy! Now get your sorry ass back out there and win one for Haldor." With reawakened passion, commitment, and questionable intelligence, I fought back an impulse to say, "Thanks Siggi, I needed that," and just went back to fishing.

11

TROUT FISHING IN DIXIE

1.

While I put on my waders and strung up a fly rod, Howard Guinn, seventy-one, sat on the tailgate of a pickup telling me something I have always wanted to know: what it was like to ride Thunder Road. Howard owns a taxicab and once owned seven. A few decades back he also owned a white two-door hardtop Chevrolet Impala with two four-barrels that he employed for running bootleg booze out of Knoxville into these northeastern Tennessee hills.

"That bitch would carry the mail," he said fondly. "I'd be over 120 miles per hour in 'er lots of times, and the heavier the load the better she'd hole the road."

Howard lost the Impala finally at a police roadblock in Morristown. He had to leave it and hit a field running. He ran ten miles and then had one of his cabs come and pick him up. "She made me a war pension 'fore I lost 'er, though," he added. "And ever trip was good even when it was bad. Just like these fishing trips with Haven."

Howard calls Haden Copeland "Haven," and Theo Copeland, "Leo," even though he has been ferrying vehicles on fishing float-trips for them for seven years. The Copelands, identical twins, are proprietors of Appalachian Angler, a guiding and outfitting service located in a little town called Valle Crucis in the Blue Ridge Mountains of western North Carolina hard by the Tennessee border, an area probably known to more people for skiing and maybe even bootlegging than for trout fishing. But Theo and Hayden are out to correct that.

Last May they invited me to come check out their fishing. I was happy to do that, but I have to admit I wasn't expecting much. Though for the past three or four decades I have given over a disproportionate amount of time to pursing trout, almost none of that time has been spent in my native South. Of course I knew that folks caught trout in such places as North Carolina, Tennessee, and Georgia, but somehow I had always pictured them using cheese balls to do so, and the trout as little, recently stocked things, as etiolated and listless as Truman Capote from the heat. Call me a snob, but the cold, clear, demanding rivers of Montana, Argentina, and New Zealand had left me feeling there was very little of trout-fishing interest below the Mason-Dixon line.

At about the same time I was invited to fish with the Copelands, I received a letter from a woman named Rebekah Stewart inviting me to sample the trout fishing at her lodge in northeast Georgia. Why not, I thought, put the two together in a mini Dixie road trip, and find out whether or not my snobbery was warranted? My wife and daughter agreed to drive up from Alabama to meet me in North Carolina, and then to go on with me from there to Georgia. If nothing else, I reckoned, we'd have a nice drive through the southern Appalachians in the most pleasant time of year there.

After Howard Guinn left to drop off a vehicle for us downriver, Haden Copeland and I went fishing. We were just below the Wilbur Dam on the Watauga River near Elizabethton, Tennessee, a two-and-a-half-hour drive from Valle Crucis. Haden had chosen for our float the six-and-a-half-mile stretch from the dam to the town of Hunter because two previous days of heavy rain had muddied his trophy stretches on the Watauga, as well as the nearby South Holston. We wade-fished the clear, slow pools just below the dam for an hour or two, casting to occasional rises, then hopped into Haden's raft around eleven and rode downstream on a release of water from the turbines.

Both this section of the Watauga and the South Holston are tailwater fisheries, and like the better-known western tailwaters, they produce abundant insect life and trout that are both fast growing and particular in their dining habits. Both rivers have predictable and prolific hatches from early March through November, and cheese balls won't even begin to cut it when the fish are keying on sulfurs or #22 Blue-Winged Olives. Rainbows and browns are stocked in both rivers but there is also good natural reproduction, and the fish here grow to respectable size by any standard. Appalachian Angler clients have caught browns up to ten pounds and rainbows to eight. Two weeks earlier, Haden told us, two clients had caught thirty fish on a half-day float, four of them over twenty inches.

"Where was that?" I asked him.

"Same float you're not catching anything on right now," he said.

That's a story I'm familiar with and have learned to rise above. It was a balmy Appalachian spring day. The Watauga riffled and pooled prettily, its banks dense with cedar, sycamore, and river birch. The farming countryside was rolling and green; the dogwoods were in bloom. And I threw a brown-and-black Woolly Bugger at the bank, mending and stripping over and over in the sweet rhythm of float fishing and couldn't have been happier with my two missed strikes and a butter-bellied seventeen-inch brown that I released at the boat.

It was Haden's brother, Theo, who introduced western-style float-fishing and tailwater fishing techniques to this area ten years before to capitalize on the unexploited potential of the Watauga and the South Holston, and I did not have to have good fishing that afternoon to see what a varied and challenging fishery the brothers have there now, or how professional an operation they run. Everything from the equipment to the shore lunch of black-ened salmon was first rate, and Haden proved to be an expert, enthusiastic guide with a sophisticated knowledge of his river and plenty of brio. "Bang it in . . . yes. *Eat* it, baby," he chattered all afternoon, rolling on his oars with body English. "There's your hole . . . *attaboy* . . . now *bang* it, baby . . ."

Give me a guy on the oars every time who wants you to catch fish and talks, yells, even moans, about it. When we took out around five, I had no doubt I had found a trouting honey hole here in these Rebel hills and a couple of good old boys who knew how to fish it. And I still had specialty of the house coming up for the next two days.

In addition to the Watauga and South Holston (which no less an expert than Gary Borger has called one of the best and most demanding trout rivers in North America), Theo and Haden offer walk-in day trips to numerous small North Carolina mountain streams for wild brown, rainbow, and brook trout, and, from May through September, an overnight float down a remote northeast-ern Tennessee river called the Nolichucky, which holds trout, musky, and a thriving population of smallmouth bass up to five pounds. Theo Copeland had told me over the phone that this

overnighter was something not to miss, and I had no trouble believing him.

Like safaris, multiday float trips are even more about who you
take them with than what you do, and we had a hard group to beat
for this one: the Copeland twins and one of their young guides
named Judson Conway, my wife, Patricia, my lip-rippin', singer-
songwriter daughter, Greta, and Greta's killer Teacup Yorkie,
Maggie—the only dog Theo and Haden had ever considered
tough enough for the Nolichucky.

We put in in three rafts around 10 a.m. The weather was flawless—bright and warm but with a western, high-altitude edge to the air that fit the feel and look of the river, which was wild and rapidy and peopleless, with sudden Class II and III drops and long, slow curves that threw open, hilly vistas in layered shades of green. We floated and chatted and sang and fished, Patricia with a spinning rod, and Greta and I in another raft with fly-rod poppers and divers. The water was clear but still high from all the recent rain, and we knew we could have caught more fish by going deep. But it was too nice a day not to fish on top and we hooked plenty of fat, olive-green, red-eyed, hard-fighting smallmouths there, releasing them all back into this jewel-like little watershed.

Around one we stopped for a shore lunch of cold barbecued chicken and slaw, then fished on down the afternoon, finding bass along stillwater banks and in backwaters. Haden lost a rainbow that he swore was over five pounds; a smallmouth that jumped four times and showed himself to be over three pounds broke me off behind a rock; and Theo told Greta and me that they had had a two hundred-fish trip on the Nolichucky last year, and that any cast might produce a muskie like the twenty-six pounder Haden had caught here: All of this adding to the sheen of possibility that lies like early sun on new good water anywhere.

Just after six we came around a big, green, curving pool and there was camp, already set up by Judson on a fine-sand beach with fields behind and the old, lush, shaggy Blue Ridge soaring over it. In July and August each year, Haden and Theo guide state-of-the-art weeklong float trips on the Kanektok River in Alaska. These boys know how to outfit an overnight. We had roomy Eureka two-man sleeping tents with cots and bags, a big kitchen tent and dining alcove with table and chairs, excellent food and wine, and a campfire after supper for stogies and stories and a tin cup of Scotch.

After eggs Benedict and oranges and cowboy coffee at seven, we pushed off for the last half of our eighteen-mile float. The morning started off sunny and fishy, but clouds soon pushed in on a front and the bass got sulky. They turned off completely in the early afternoon when it started to thunder and then to pour, but we fished all the way out, enjoying even the rain. We loaded the rafts and gear onto the vehicles in a sheeting downpour just a mile or so above Davy Crockett's birthplace, and, soaking wet, every one of us regretted getting off the Nolichucky.

Theo and Haden and the seven young guides they employ have some sixty miles of that wonderful river to fish. They also have twenty-three miles of the Watauga, fourteen miles of the South Holston, and a good number of walk-in streams full of wild mountain trout. They know all that water cold and have brought to the fishing of it zeal, style, and the most sophisticated trouting techniques. And best of all, they have it practically to themselves and their clients—perhaps because too many dummies believe there is no trout fishing of interest below the Mason-Dixon line. As Howard Guinn would say, even when that's bad it's good.

2.

Greta was already awake when I went down to the lower-floor bedroom of our cabin to rouse her. Still in bed and staring combatively at the ceiling, she said, "So who caught the fifteen pounder?"

"What are you talking about?" I asked her.

"I just heard you tell Mom upstairs that somebody already caught a fifteen-pound rainbow on a four-weight rod this morning, and it's not even eight o'clock. What are they doing fishing our water?"

"First, I didn't say that. Second, it's fifteen minutes *past* eight, so get up."

"You didn't just say that, about the fifteen pounder on the four-weight?"

"Nope," I said. "And get up. I've got some coffee going up-stairs."

My daughter stared at the ceiling, her competitive juices cool-ing. Since she was an infant, she has had enough of that juice to boil crawfish for all of Louisiana. "I must've dreamed it, then," she said with a grin and got out of bed. "Maybe Toots sent me that dream."

"Toots" was Greta's name for my father, a man who loved fish-ing, and particularly fly fishing for trout, to near hysteria, and who passed along that same pitch of angling passion to both me and Greta. When I was about ten years old, Toots gave me my first fly rod—a six-foot, one-piece, split-cane heart-stopper, made by Or-vis, with which I caught my first and many subsequent trout. I had come across that rod a few weeks earlier—a serene and lovely grande dame in a closet full of young, sexy graphites—and decided to bring it along on this part of our southern road trip for Greta to fish with. I couldn't remember what weight line the rod threw, so I tested it out with a variety of lines, settling on a double-tapered #4, which the little rod launched daintily and at surprising dis-tance.

After our coffee, I presented the rod to Greta and—knowing her tendency not to play around with fish—asked her to be careful with it. "There really *might* be some big trout in this river, though I'm sure nothing like the stories we've heard, and this is basically a bluegill rod. Just don't reef on it. It's about twenty years older than you are."

With our guides, Marty Long and Bill Kelly, we walked down a trail behind the main lodge building to the Soque River, then followed it downstream along another trail to Long Pool. It was a snappy blue May morning, warming into the 70s. The river twisted and chuckled from riffle to pool, a happy, exquisite little thing that tugged sweetly at my legs when I waded into it. There was not much happening with insects yet, so Greta and I both tied on small olive Woolly Buggers with bead heads. I stood knee-deep in the river watching her wade out to a boulder fifty yards above me, climb up on the boulder, and begin covering a big, deep, slow-water pool. I watched her casting—the cane rod stopping high at two o'clock, bending to the butt as it pulled the line forward into a cone-shaped loop over her head, then stopping again suddenly at ten o'clock with a motion from her hand like driving a nail, the green line rolling out straight, dropping the fly without fuss into the pool's tenderloin—and thought that if there is anything more complexly satisfying than casting a fly rod well, it would have to be watching someone you love do it.

On my third cast into Long Pool, I hooked a fish that jumped on the strike, showing itself to be the biggest brown trout I have ever seen outside of New Zealand. After I tired it, I lifted the fish, a male of eight pounds and change, one hand around its tail, the other under its belly, and shouted for Greta to have a look at this astonishing thing, but she was hard into a fish of her own.

She stood on the boulder with the little cane rod bent alarmingly, its reel nowhere in sight. Marty was wading up to his chest out ahead of her carrying a long-handled net, and just at the end of the pool, before the river dropped to a falls, a trout broke water and thrashed. It couldn't be as big as it looked, I told myself, and hoped for the sake of my first fly rod that it wasn't. The scene upriver—the evidently gigantic, thrashing fish, the guide wading after it to his armpits, my daughter with the antique, reel-less rod

straining overhead—had a surreal, dreamlike look to it, as did the
pristine downstream landscape of river-crowding trees, shrubs,
and ferns, white-flecked riffles, and rock-carved pools. At that moment it took some effort to remember that I was in northeast
Georgia, of all places, and to make that remembering parse. Could
that really have been an eight-pound brown trout I just released?
And what on earth could Greta be hooked up to? Was Toots down
there on the boulder with her?

Well, who knew? I thought as I waded up to Greta: We were,
after all, at a place called Brigadoon.

Brigadoon, you might remember, is the name of a magical and
unleavable land that rises out of the mist, holding your most secret
and precious fantasies—which in Gene Kelly's case took the leggy
form of Cyd Charisse in the eponymous 1930s musical comedy.
And it is the name Rebekah Stewart chose for the fifteen-acre
property in the foothills of the Blue Ridge Mountains near Clarks-
ville, Georgia, that she found on her thirtieth birthday, maybe in
the mist, on her way back to Atlanta from a wedding.

Rebekah—now more than a decade older, with a model's body,
a smoky Southern voice, and a light rein on her surprising life—
had grown up in Atlanta, moved to New York at twenty-three, and
made a killing there working for Smith Barney as an institutional
investment consultant. On the drive back to Atlanta from the wedding, in between bad marriages of her own, she saw a For Sale
sign on the fifteen acres, stumbled down a bank in high heels to
the Soque River, and fell in love with something more dependable
than a man. She bought the property the next morning, and for
the next year lived on it in a tent and commuted to New York. She
would dress each morning by a kerosene lantern in a Chanel suit,
drive the hour and a half to Atlanta, take a plane to New York, do

business all day, with lunch at 21, and be back in her tent at night.
After a couple of years of that, she moved back to Atlanta to work
out of the Smith Barney office there, and then, a year later, when
her mother sold the apartment in Atlanta where Rebekah lived,
and Hurricane Hugo destroyed her house in St. Croix, she replaced the tent with a sumptuous house on the east bank of the
Soque. After a few years of living there, she decided that she
needed a full-time gardener and that, to finance his salary, she
would turn her northeast Georgia home into a trout lodge. If that
sounds to you like an oxymoronic idea, and one highly unlikely to
appeal to a seasoned venture capitalist, it is only because you
haven't met either the Soque River or Rebekah. The latter simply
does what she decides to do; the former, astonishingly, happens to
be one of the most ideal trout habitats in the county.

Browns and rainbows were introduced to the Soque in the first
few decades of the twentieth century and flourished there into a
large and thriving population of stream-bred trout, many of them
of eye-popping size. This is due in part to the river's large biomass
of insects (caddis, mayflies, and stoneflies), and to a steep rock
face along much of the river's west bank that keeps the hot afternoon sun off the water and creates deep ledge holding pools for
the fish. It is also due to Rebekah's diligent nurturing of the trout
and the mile and a half of river she owns. From her tenting days
onward, this woman, who doesn't fish and never intends to, has
built spawning redds, put in structure, and shaped pools, under-
pruned the banks, and cleared out springs. She also feeds the
trout, more to hold them there (and away from the public
stretches of river where they tend to be killed and eaten) than to
fatten them up, because her feeding program in the insect-rich
Soque provides less than 1 percent of the trout's diet.

And hold them there she has: There are now four thousand to
forty-two hundred trout per mile in Rebekah's water, a better

population than that in all but a very few of the legendary Rocky Mountain rivers. And (read this twice) the average weight of those fish is six and a half pounds. The largest brown trout caught (and released, as all fish are at Brigadoon) from Rebekah's twelve pools weighed seventeen pounds; the largest rainbow, seventeen and a half. And fish of both species of over ten pounds are caught regularly. If you have never heard of the Soque before (as I had not before Rebekah's letter), it is only because it is a well-guarded secret among the closed-mouthed 90 percent-return clients who visit Brigadoon. I just recently learned, for example, that two of the best and most widely traveled trout anglers I know caught the biggest trout of their lives there.

In the lodge itself, Rebekah has created as inviting a habitat for anglers as she has in her river for trout. The main lodge building, which sleeps eight in four bedrooms, is fitted out with antique furniture, fine books, oriental rugs, and art. There are two more bedrooms in a wood-and-stone cabin that looks like Ralph Lauren designed and furnished it, and two more in a house on an adjoining property that Rebekah recently acquired. Cocktails and hors d'ouevres are served each evening after fishing, as elegantly as at an Argentine estancia on a stone patio by the river, where, as everywhere at Brigadoon, there is nothing to see but what gladdens the eye and brings joy and solace to the contemplative troutfisherman's soul. A groomed trail runs between Rebekah's pools among mountain laurel, hemlocks, and rhododendrons, with dogwood and azaleas winking at you through the shadowy green, and teak benches are placed here and there for an after-trout cigar. Because Brigadoon is surrounded on all four sides by the seventy thousand-acre Chattahoochee National Forest and the lodge accepts no more than ten rods at a time, you can smoke that cigar without fear of offending anyone.

In fact, Greta, Patricia, and I had the place to ourselves for the two days we were there, and it felt a little like owning our own eighteen-hole championship golf course (an analogy, I admit, that occurred to me after learning that the ESPN show *Fly Fishing America* had called Brigadoon "the Augusta National of fly fishing"). Indeed, though Rebekah's fish are fed, they are anything but pets and are as chary about being caught as big fish in small streams are anywhere. You can forget the trout-pellet patterns here. When the olive Buggers quit working, Greta and I caught fish on Muddlers with a Prince nymph dropper for a while, then had lots of dry-fly refusals during a mayfly hatch until we went to a #18 Parachute Adams. On the second day, nothing worked in a light drizzle for a while until we tried emergers.

The pools are beautifully defined at Brigadoon, and you see four- to ten-pound fish lying everywhere, but they are nobody's fools and your small-stream casting and mending skills had better be above par. Also, your fish-playing skills: Rebekah's well-mothered fish fight like Crips and Bloods, and, according to her, of the ten to twelve of them hooked by an average angler in a day, more than half release themselves.

Which seemed inevitable in the case of the trout Greta had hooked while standing on the boulder. When I waded up to her, she was chest-deep in the pool, holding the one-piece cane rod high overhead and playing the fish with her left hand on a line that disappeared into the water toward its reel somewhere at the bottom of the pool. Marty was making futile stabs with his net at a huge circling dorsal fin.

"Uh, where is your reel, Greta?" I asked, as if for the time of day.

"In the *water*, Dad. It fell off the ridiculous teeny little rings on this reel seat. Do you see the size of that fish? *What am I doing with this wimpy little rod*? It's my *dream*, Dad—a fifteen-pounder on a four-weight rod, only this rod, of course, has to be a hundred years old!"

"It's a family heirloom, not a rod. Oh my God, you're *reef ing* on it, Greta . . ."

Just then Marty made another stab and, miraculously, the trout of Greta's dream was in the net.

I would tell you that it was a lovely hen rainbow of not fifteen but close to twelve pounds, the biggest rainbow Marty had ever seen caught at Brigadoon, certainly the biggest ever caught there by a woman, and possibly the women's Georgia state record, but that would be triply bragging—on my daughter, my first fly rod, and on the superlative trout fishing I always knew we had right here in Dixie.

12

DAUGHTERS OF THE RIVER GODDESS

For me, as for many other slaves to fly fishing, the money moment of the sport, the one that justifies all the often-considerable expense and frustration that delivers you to it, is the take: the instant when a fish grabs your fly (ideally on the surface of the water) and you are suddenly, astonishingly, tight to the primordial throbbings of something trying to save its life. For addicts like myself, even a lifetime of fishing doesn't dull that rush. Long after we have quit caring about the number of fish we catch, their size, or whether we land them or not, we will travel a long way for a good top-water take—even halfway around the world, as I recently did, for a legendary one.

The vast blue sky and tawny landscape could have been Montana in another century, like maybe the fourteenth, and the merry little Eg River was clear and twinkling in the sun. I had been casting an enormous imitation-rodent fly called a Verminator into the sweet declivities of the Eg's banks and twitching it back seductively for hours with no bites. And, having drifted into my normal ox-like casting reverie, I was not at all prepared when the take finally came. Nor could I have been. The water exploded around the Verminator, and there—hanging theatrically in the air with its lipstick-red gills aflare and all but the tail of its three-foot body out of the water—was a *Hucho hucho taimen,* arguably the most thrilling taker in the business.

The fish fought nobly and all that, and after a while it was in the net. Local shamanists believed the taimen to be the daughter of the River Goddess, and a Buddhist sutra holds that for every one of them killed, 999 human souls will suffer. Not that Genghis Khan would have cared: He would have bonked this fish on the head and taken it home for supper. That hardly being an option here, my boat mates and I simply stared at the huge, melancholy-eyed creature, took a few photos, and carefully released it after writing down the number on the green tag embedded in its back. This daughter of the River Goddess was taimen number 0747, last caught two inches shorter, almost exactly one year ago, and three river miles from where I caught it.

Mongolia, I was learning, was full of paradoxes and here was one more. The river we were on was as wild and remote as any on the planet—you simply cannot *go* anywhere to fish that is farther away from everything modern. And yet nowhere on earth could that taimen have been brought into a boat containing more au courant environmental, scientific, and socio-religious concerns for its welfare than ours did.

The largest and possibly most ancient member of the Salmonid family of salmon and trout, taimen can grow to more than six-feet long and over two hundred pounds. Either exceedingly rare or completely extirpated in most of the Eurasian watersheds it once called home, the fish hangs on to survival as a species now only in a few river systems in Siberia and Mongolia. And even in the remotest of those systems, like the Eg-Uur watershed of north-western Mongolia where I was fishing, the taimen is increasingly vulnerable to poaching and mining-related depredations of its habitat. But on the Eg-Uur, the fish has some determined champions, and three of them were in the boat with me that day.

Dan Vermillion is a strapping, affable young man from Livingston, Montana, and owner with his brother, Jeff, of Sweetwater Travel, a fly-fishing outfitting and booking agency. In 1997, with a Mongolian partner, the brothers set up a fixed base camp on the Uur River and began offering taimen fishing to adventurous sports on 120 miles of that river and the Eg, into which it flows. Though there are also lenok (imagine a sort of rainbow trout with a carp's mouth), grayling, and pike in those rivers, it is the taimen's take and size—the camp record weighed over seventy pounds—that induces anglers to make the very long journey there and spend north of $5,000 dollars a week to fish. Early on in their operation, Dan and Jeff realized that poaching and mining were escalating threats to their bread-and-butter fish and had begun to consider ways of providing it with some sort of long-term protection, when out of the blue one of the other men in our boat called them. He had heard about their taimen program, he said, and liked their conservation concerns—might a million dollars help?

Bright, voluble, and determined as a Jack Russell terrier, Jeff Leiber has loved all things Mongolian since he spent two years in the early 1990s as the first Peace Corps volunteer to that country. He learned the language and began doing business development there after he left the Peace Corps. In 1999 it was as an investment officer of the International Finance Corporation, the private-lending arm of the World Bank, that he contacted Dan and Jeff, kicking off what has to be one of the most unusual collaborations in the history of fisheries conservation.

The men began a Mongolian NGO called the Taimen Conservation Fund that brought together local communities, government agencies, and tourist companies to create and implement a taimen-management program for the Eg-Uur drainage. Since

2003 the fund has established environmental-education work-
shops for locals, imposed a taimen catch-and-release-only policy
on the two rivers, hired watershed residents to act as antipoaching
wardens, and funded a five-year research program utilizing scientists from three American universities to conduct the most exten-
sive study of taimen ever undertaken. One of those scientists, Zeb
Hogan, a fisheries biologist from the University of Nevada, Reno,
was the third man in our boat. He and his coworkers tag and
surgically implant radio transmitters into taimen to monitor the
fish's range and seasonal movement patterns and come up with
informed conclusions about the nature and sustainability of the
Eg-Uur fishery. Among their gleanings so far: a scant population
of only one forty-inch, or large, taimen per mile of river, and size-

age correlations that put the thirty-eight-inch fish I caught at between twenty and twenty-five years old, and a five-footer at over fifty.

Another major contributor to the well-being of the aged and lonely taimen of the Eg and Uur was in our boat in spirit that day if not in her blonde, effervescent person. Betsy Gaines Quammen, a Montanan with a long history of conservation work, heard about the Taimen Fund as it was being conceived. After coming to Mongolia to check it out, it seemed to her that the best way to ensure the long-term effectiveness of a conservation ethic for the rivers was to involve in its creation the interest and commitment of the local Buddhist community. For over four hundred years the predominant religion of Mongolia, and one that places a high value on all things living, Buddhism, she reckoned, might marry faith and conservation where they needed marrying—in the minds and hearts of the townspeople and nomadic herders who live in the watershed area. And who better, she further reckoned, to pay for such a marriage than the deep-pocketed foreign anglers who stood to benefit by it?

In 2004 she started an organization called the Tributary Fund with donations, mostly from those foreign anglers, that now amount to over $500,000. With that funding she has established an outreach and education program that works with Eg-Uur watershed schools and helps to educate young monks. And she has spectacularly rebuilt, near the Sweetwater camp on the Uur, a Buddhist monastery destroyed during Mongolia's Soviet era, to be used as an environmental clearinghouse and meditation center where the River Goddess's daughters might be pondered and appreciated, hopefully long into the future.

Even if it continues to flourish under all this attention, the taimen of the Eg-Uur will never be an attractive quarry for the numbers fishermen. My buddy Hakan Stenlund caught a small one after I released mine, and Jeff Leiber lost one. Along with a few more the three of us lost or failed to hook over that day and the one before, that was our total taimen tally, and that was about normal. In an average stay at one of the two Sweetwater camps, one on each of the rivers, an angler can hope to raise three to five fish a day and catch perhaps ten to fifteen in seven days of fishing.

Compensations must often be groped for at high-priced angling destinations where hookups are few, but there are no shortage of them ready to hand at the Vermillion operation. There are the unforgettable takes, of course, and the size of the fish: A fair number of the ten to fifteen taimen you catch in a week will likely be over forty inches, with one perhaps over fifty inches. And whenever you tire of lobbing Verminators, and Chernobyl Squirrels on big rods, you can take out a four-weight, tie on a small dry, and catch eager-to-eat grayling and lenok up to twenty-four inches. Moreover, you will be doing that on rivers as lovely as any in the world, more often than not in perfect mountain weather, and in a landscape of surpassing beauty and uncompromised wildness, where broad grassland steppes lap up against sage and tan mountains striped with taiga forests of Siberian larch and pine that are home to foxes and wolves, bear, moose, elk, and roe deer. And after a day of marinating your soul in all this natural splendor, you will return to a comfortable camp that consists of a log dining building and five *gers*—the round felt tents of Mongolian nomads—each accommodating two people with plenty of room, good cots, and a woodstove.

On our last night at the Uur camp, a "barbecue" of mutton steamed on hot rocks inside a thing that looked like a milk can was followed by a concert of traditional Mongolian music. Young Rocky Mountain guides, four Texan anglers, my boat mates, and I sat—some of us still in our fishing long johns, eyes drooping, holding wineglasses—and listened to three women and two men, dressed in embroidered silk costumes, play haunting pentatonic music from the Chinese courts of Kublai Khan on a collection of instruments so exotic I had no idea any of them existed.

Toward the end of the concert, one of the male performers broke into *hoomie*, or throat singing, the hair-raising concatenation of sound (at different times like the warbling of ravens, like a synthesizer run amok, like tree frogs; and at no time like anything you can imagine being made by the human voice) that is created by breath control and a fluttering tongue down in some mysterious part of the diaphragm. His wife accompanied him, her alabaster fingers flying over a sort of square, horse-headed fiddle couched in her lap, a red smile playing over her oval face. The combined sound had the smell of centuries of dung fires, and mutton fat in it, and the colors of camel hair and the Eternal Blue Sky sacred to Mongolian shamanists. It had in it something so profoundly, simply, and valuably from a nearly lost time and place that it seemed to one, perhaps tired and overserved, member of the audience that all of Mongolia ought to have a green tag implanted in its back.

Once (under the Khan successors to Genghis) the hub of the largest empire the world has ever known, Mongolia today is bordered by China to the south and Russia to the north and is roughly the size of Alaska. In 1924 it became the world's second communist country, as the Mongolian People's Republic, and for the next six decades it functioned, not without suffering, as a Soviet satellite. Under the purges of Stalin in the 1930s, over sixty thousand of its Buddhist monks were executed, imprisoned, or forced into exile, and more than 600 of its 770 temples and monasteries were destroyed. After the unraveling of the Soviet Union, Mongolia declared itself decolonized from Russia in 1990 and amended its

constitution to allow multiparty elections. The price of this democ-
ratization was a near economic collapse following the pullout of
Russian investment and infrastructure, and the country has struggled ever since to dig out from under it, pretty much grasping at
any helping hand offered.

And many are. The capital city of Ulaanbaatar these days is
aswarm with various multinational groups eagerly interested in
leading Mongolia out of the Dark Ages and into affluence and
modernity by developing its considerable natural resources, as
well as the last wilderness areas left in Asia. Gleaming new hotels
rise beside gray Soviet-era housing projects. Coal-fired power
plants darken the air over *ger* suburbs, and American tour opera-
tors, Chinese and Australian businessmen, and Canadian mining
engineers walk the traffic-jammed streets with cell phones to their
ears, cheek by jowl with red-robed Buddhist monks and felt-
booted yak herders.

About half of Mongolia's 2.8 million population still live partially or entirely nomadic lives, but that percentage is changing as
rapidly as the economy responsible for it. Mining—mostly for copper and gold—will soon overtake animal husbandry as the country's biggest industry. And that "progress," inevitably, is coming at
a cost. Mongolia's three-hundred-plus mines have so far polluted
more than two dozen of its river basins, and many of its forests are
steadily being lost to a growing need for wood to build houses.
Throughout the country, pastureland and canyons are threatened
by planned hydropower stations. And an increasing, mostly Chinese, demand for meat and fur has caused dozens of animals, from
musk deer to marmots, to become endangered.

Fortunately, among the new and hungry hoard of individuals
and corporations now jostling to invest themselves in Mongolia's
future are a few tag-monitors—socio-conservationists, you might
call them—who care about and study the quality and sustainability

of the country's rush into the twenty-first century, and who are working to preserve what is unique and irreplaceable in its natural resources and ancient culture. The Tributary and Taimen Conservation Funds are solidly in this camp, and so are the people who operate a remarkable resort in the Gobi Desert called Three Camel Lodge.

That lodge is located in Omnogov, or South Gobi, the least-populated province (0.3 people per square kilometer) of the least-populated country in the world, but that hardly seems to concern the lodge owners. Opened for its unlikely business three years ago at the base of a volcanic outcrop overlooking a pure and unbroken expanse of the dun-colored high desert steppe that makes up 90 percent of the Gobi Desert, the lodge is most assuredly what it claims to be: "Mongolia's Premiere Luxury Expedition Camp." As well, it is a uniquely satisfying experiment in blending comfortable outdoors adventure with ecological and cultural responsibility. The resort complex consists of a stunning main lodge, built mortise and tenon of local wood and stone by local craftsmen along the lines of a Buddhist temple; a house-sized dining *ger* designed after the Great Khan's feast tents; and thirty sleeping *gers*, some with en suite stone bathrooms, that come with posh beds, woodstoves, and beautifully hand-painted furniture. Three Camel sleeps you luxuriously, wines and dines you very well indeed, entertains you with traditional music and dancing, and even Mongolian massages you at the end of a long day of adventuring. It also runs itself on wind and solar power, employs over 90 percent local people, makes its sumptuous four-course meals from organic food raised and grown locally, funds and organizes Gobi conservation and cultural appreciation clubs for local children, and serves as a base for scientific research and wildlife monitoring in the desert. Tell *that* to your local Four Seasons.

In addition, the lodge can supply you in three days, as it did Hakan Stenlund and me, with daytime outings of sufficient variety, piquancy, and visual splendor to make for a lifetime of memories.

Outfitted with an expedition vehicle, a driver, and a charming English-speaking guide named Bayana, we hiked at dawn in the spectacular mountains of 2.7 million-hectare Three Beauties National Park, looking among its ragged eight-thousand-foot peaks for the wolves, argali sheep, ibex, and snow leopards that call them home, and followed that with another, staggeringly lovely, hike up the precipitous Yolyn Am Valley to the world's only year-round desert glacier. The following dawn saw us walking sand dunes toward a rising sun, where striding along the soft, tawny undulations felt to me after ten days of sleep deprivation so gloriously like traversing the recumbent back of a gigantic sunbathing Cindy Crawford that there was nothing for it but to throw my arms wide at the top of one of her buttocks and break into my workmanlike rendition of "O Sole Mio."

We shared snuff, yogurt, and fermented mare's milk with a nomadic family in their *ger*, then rode their camels to the Flaming Cliffs, an orange-red outcropping of seventy-million-year-old wind-fluted buttes, where in 1924 the first dinosaur eggs were discovered. As we walked beneath the cliffs looking for fossils, our camels chewed their bits and watched us with long-lashed, blasé Upper East Side eyes.

And on our last afternoon, Hakan, Bayana, and I were led by our driver, Wednesday, to a newly discovered petroglyph site in the Zeoolon Mountains, northeast of the lodge. After a steep climb we topped out on a summit of black volcanic rock. Forming a rough circle there, twenty or thirty stones had been etched over four thousand years ago with drawings of camels, ibex, gazelles, and a few human figures. The convoluted mountains surrounding us were a dragon green, and below, the vast, subtle, and vulnerable Gobi stretched out endlessly in every direction, with blue mirages to the south and patches of sage blossoms and wild onion showing yellow against the sparse olive grassland. Nowhere in all that vista, yet, was a copper mine.

Perhaps the only word to make its way into English usage from Mongolian is an exclamation of mutual encouragement and exhortation to courage used by Genghis Khan's troops as they rode into battle. On the way back down the mountain, well away from the real deal, I carved my own petroglyph into a tall black stone, and it seemed a fitting symbol for modern Mongolia: a taimen at the take.

"Hurray!" I wrote in a bubble above its head.

13

DEEP LUXURY IN DREAMTIME

Here is Genesis according to the Gagudju Aborigines, of Northern Australia, who as a people have been around almost long enough to know:

The world has always existed; but long ago, before time could be measured, it had no particulars or shape, and there was no life on land or in the seas. Below the surface of the Earth, however, the Creator Spirits, the Ancestors, lay dormant and ripe with the potential for all life. On the morning of the First Day, the beginning of Dreamtime, these Ancestors awoke, rose, and shook the clay from themselves. A female Creator named Warramurrungundji came out of the sea onto land carrying a digging stick and a dilly bag full of yams and water lilies and other sustaining plants. She gave birth to the first humans and gave them language. She planted the yams and other plants, and then walked around plunging her digging stick into the ground to create water holes. The other Ancestors, thousands of them, opened their mouths and called out, "I am!" "I am Bandicoot," said one. "I am Wallaby," said another. "I am Honey Ant . . . Snake . . . Lizard." Then these Ancestors began to walk, and as they walked they called out the names of things—paperback swamp, billabong, crocodile, sand dune—calling these things into existence by naming them and weaving the names into Songs. The Ancestors walked all over the Earth during the Dreamtime, singing up the particulars of the world and wrapping the land and the seas in a giant musical score, a web of songlines. They created everything that is and can be. Some of it—such as all the things so important to you and me, our guns and cold beers and airplanes and sailboats—they left beneath the Earth's surface, dozing, waiting to be called up as needed.

When the entire Earth and everything in it was sung, the Ancestors were understandably tired. Some sank back into the Earth. Some lay down and became rocks and ridges and hills and water holes, and they remain those things today and for all time, which is why every feature of the earth is sacred to the Aborigines.

In no place are those features more sacred than on the Cobourg Peninsula, the wild, staghorn-shaped cape onto which Warramur-rungundji is said to have come ashore carrying her dilly bag and digging stick. That peninsula—extending some fifty miles into the Arafura Sea from Arnhem Land, the northernmost part of Australia's Northern Territory—is also almost certainly the place where the first human Australians came ashore (if they were not in fact sung into being), after island-hopping through Indonesia from southern China or India between fifty and a hundred thousand years ago.

These people were among the earliest Homo sapiens, and they were the world's first navigators. For tens of thousands of years after arriving in Australia, they were the most advanced people on Earth. They invented the first technology and they were the first artists. Their culture had been around for at least forty thousand years by the time the world's other people first settled in villages and began planting crops. However it was originated, the Australian Aboriginal culture is almost inconceivably ancient, by thousands of years the oldest continuous culture on Earth.

For all those millennia the Aborigines lived very lightly on the Cobourg Peninsula merging their nomadic lives into the land and the seasons. The first European to visit the peninsula was Pieter Pieterszoon, on the Dutch ship *Batavia* in 1636. The British tried three settlements there, deserting the last one in 1849, and leaving as the only enduring sign of their presence the water buffalo, Timor ponies, Sambar deer, and banteng cattle they introduced. In 1963 the peninsula was designated a wildlife sanctuary, which subsequently became the twenty-two-thousand-square-kilometer Gurig National Park, home of outrageously prolific, named particulars, old and new songlines laid down through a wilderness as unscathed and unchanged as it is still possible to find on this good Earth.

There are no towns, no paved roads on the Cobourg Peninsula. But there could be, of course. High-rise hotels and golf courses could also have been sung up there from under the Earth's crust to profit the thirty or so traditional Aboriginal owners of the land that is now Gurig National Park. Instead, in 1987 a Melbourne company called Lowell Capital Ltd. proposed to those owners a small-scale, ecologically friendly but unspeakably deluxe "wilderness habitat" to be developed on ten square kilometers of the park, which would be leased to the developers for fifty years. The landowners liked the sound of that and, thus, to the tune of $8.5 million, Seven Spirit Bay, which may be the world's finest wilderness lodge, was sung into being on April 1, 1990, on the Cobourg Peninsula.

After one visit to this lodge, it is impossible not to believe it is exactly what the Ancestors had in mind for the place all along.

A visit to Seven Spirit Bay begins in Darwin, capital of the Northern Territory. That territory is two and a half times the size of
Texas and has a population of fewer than 150,000 people, about
half of whom live in Darwin. The territory's desolate person-to-
land ratio gives Darwin a whistling-in-the-dark cheerfulness, a pioneer hardiness and candor and cowboy swagger that might remind

you, as it did me, of Anchorage, Alaska, another outpost in the middle of a haunting Big Empty.

Like Anchorage, Darwin is a jumping-off town for the wilds surrounding it, and most of that jumping is done in small planes. After a night at the friendly Beaufort Hotel, my wife, Patricia, and I took a cab out to the private terminal for Executive Air Charter. A hostess brought us coffee and fruit juice, and we sat in spiffy rattan furniture listening to classical music while our chartered Beechcraft Baron was loaded. The flight to the Cobourg Peninsula over Van Diemen Gulf—with its dugongs and manta rays, its false killer whales and sharks and saltwater crocodiles, its unequivocal remoteness—took forty-five minutes. We landed on a little red clay strip cut out of the bush and were met there by a Toyota LandCruiser, rigged safari-style with two bench seats in the back, in which we were driven for thirty minutes more to Seven Spirit Bay.

If you have not already sensed from the flight over Van Diemen Gulf in exactly how exotic a place you are, this drive will announce it to you loudly and clearly. I happen to love wilderness lodges and have visited them in more than a few places around the world. By definition, the site of any such lodge is exotic, but some are more so than others and none is more so than the Cobourg Peninsula. Your first experience with the bush there and its rushing, dappling light, its giant red termite mounds, woollybutt and screw palm trees, kookaburras and bouncing wallabies, and frill-necked lizards and peering Timor ponies can make you feel trapped in the pages of a Dr. Seuss book. In such circumstances the mind clutches for some familiar frame of reference. All mine could come up with were the drab pine woods and red clay of south Alabama; and indeed, the humid, velvety touch of the air did sort of make you want to go sit in a rocker under a sweetgum tree and open up a can of sardines.

Instead, upon arriving at the lodge, we sat at a polished jarrah wood table set with linen and Wedgewood in a high-ceilinged, air-conditioned dining room with apricot walls, surrounded by potted trees and enormous vases of flowers. And we ate, not sardines at all, but tiger prawns with coriander, asparagus and cherry tomato salads, and an exquisite mango and ginger sorbet.

The crisp, lovely dining room at Seven Spirit Bay is part of the "social hub," or main building, which also has a bar and lounge, a photographic darkroom, a reception area and shop, and—connected by a walkway—a library/conference room. Skirting the rear of this main building are an outdoor dining terrace and broad, partially shaded, decks that front a lagoon-like freshwater pool edged with stones and ferns.

Standing on the terrace in full postprandial glow, looking beyond the pool through a little copse of palms to a white new-moon beach embracing a tongue of blue sea, the weary traveler immediately senses that all is well at this place. And that sense can only be amplified when he and his wife are taken to their "habitat," the ungainly word used at Seven Spirit Bay to describe the eucalyptus-nested hexagonal bungalows in which guests are housed. There are twenty-four of these little buildings, each sited for maximum privacy, for views of the bay, and for exposure to the sights and sounds of the bush, with five of the walls made only of screen and adjustable louvers. On the outside, the bungalows are spare and unobtrusive; inside, they are spacious, clean-lined, and stylish, with twin ceiling fans over queen-size beds, stocked refrigerator minibars, and satellite telephone with which you could call your office in Toledo if for some unimaginable reason you should want to do so.

Delighted with these digs, Patricia and I put down our bags and went to look at our bathroom. To do that at Seven Spirit Bay you walk twenty steps or so down a path to a separate structure that is enclosed enough for privacy, but otherwise open air, planted with creepers and ferns, tiled in shiny white, and stocked with designer toiletries. Later that evening, bathing for dinner in what could pass for Eden's own shower stall, I watched a frog hop from the tile floor into the ferns, and it occurred to me that this fascinating little bathroom was a paradigm for Seven Spirit Bay itself. But more on that in a minute.

Bob the banteng bull grazed in the bush near our bungalow. Sharing that bush with him were various other animals, ten kinds of lizards, five kinds of frogs, nine kinds of snakes, and over twenty makes of birds. Ubiquitous was a family of wallabies—a big, indifferent-looking male and his mate who carried a joey in her pouch. This baby and mother stared at Patricia and me on our first walk over to the main building with exactly the same high- and low-beam expressions of startled assessment. Everywhere at Seven Spirit Bay nature is invited to the party. Everywhere you go you walk through glimpses and sounds of creatures as though through a fine rain. And that, says Basil Noonan, the lodge's genial manager, is the point. What he and his staff of fifteen quite successfully do, with a minimum of taxing ecotourism fanfare and verbiage, is to put guests in the middle of an ancient and interesting wilderness environment, provide opportunities for them to learn about it, and then leave them alone in sublime creature comfort to enjoy it. The unique triumph of the place, one realizes within hours of arriving there, is in the delicate balances it strikes—of style and scale with the landscape, and of nature with nurture. That first night at the lodge, while washing my scalp with scented shampoo and looking forward to an Australian cabernet with the grilled loin of buffalo I had seen on the hand-printed evening's menu in the bar, I watched the aforementioned frog hop across the gleaming white tiles of our bathroom and realized with soaring anticipation for the next few days that we had landed in a thrillingly unlikely oxymoron: a truly luxurious wilderness lodge.

Each morning in the lobby of Seven Spirit Bay a board announces a menu of activities for the day. There is no shortage of these. A typical day's options might include two or three different kinds of fishing; offshore sailing on the *Touche*, a fifty-foot ocean-racing yacht; a half-day trip to the bony ruins of Victoria Settlement, the last British attempt to colonize the peninsula; a mountain bike ride along banteng cattle trails; exploring bays and beaches in one of the lodge's numerous and various-size motor launches; an overnight stay in a tented bush camp; and various walks—bird and wildlife watching walks, coral reef walks, beach walks, swamp walks, and bush walks—all of them accompanied by a trained naturalist who will explain to you what you are seeing, naming things right and left as ardently as any Ancestor. Two or three times a week all this activity is capped off just before dinner by a slide-show lecture on the flora, fauna, and history of the area.

What you will never see listed on the activity board, notwithstanding the fact that the lodge is surrounded by some of the most beautiful beaches and inviting ocean water on earth, is anything that involves swimming, diving, or even wading in that ocean. There are a number of very good reasons for that, all of them inhabiting the Arafura Sea. Starting with the smallest of them, there are deadly stonefish to step on and poisonous sea snakes to bite you. Then, in some months, there are box jellyfish, known as stingers, whose appallingly toxic tentacles can cause immediate cardiac and respiratory arrest. And finally, there are bull sharks and ocean-roaming saltwater crocodiles up to twenty feet long.

On our first morning at the lodge, I looked over at a small, lapping turquoise bay, maybe a hundred yards across, and ventured to Myles Mulvay, the lodge's naturalist, that I thought I might just swim across it and back to cool off.

"Mmmm, I wouldn't do that," he said. But then he squinted at the bay and scientific curiosity almost got the better of him. "I do wonder how far you'd get before something ate you . . . maybe halfway across? Probably not."

Over the course of our visit, we took a number of totally absorbing walks in the Cobourg Peninsula bush with Myles, who was encyclopedic there without being pedantic. It is very old land, this land of Aboriginal Ancestors—at least sixty-five million years old. At one time, like all very old land, it harbored a bestiary of monsters, both real and imagined—the Thylacaleo, or marsupial lion; Tasmanian devils and tigers; a perentie lizard thirty feet long; the Boly-yas, a flop-eared and vengeful Aboriginal boogeyman that ate human flesh but left the bones; the Manu-manu, fanged and Yeti-like, who moved underground and carried off strangers. Now it is a far more hospitable place than its neighboring sea, with only a few (mostly nocturnal) snakes and strychnine trees to worry about, and a nonthreatening bestiary made up primarily of the feral pigs, buffalo, ponies, and cattle introduced by the English, and native bandicoots, wallabies, and dingos.

We saw all of these animals and had them named for us, along with ghost gum, a tree the color of sea foam; bloodwood, ironwood, and milkwood; kerosene trees, Carpentaria palms. We got a short course in some of the Aborigines' "bush tucker" such as green plum, cocky apple, and billy-goat plum. We learned how the Aborigines would follow seed cases on a vine to yams, fingered and smelled the lemongrass they used to put their babies to sleep, and ate a few of the tart green ants they favored, guessing they might be better with tequila. We watched crested cockatoos and kookaburras clatter through the skinned, ghostly eucalyptus, treed a two-foot frill-necked lizard in a pandanus palm, and sat by a billabong in a paperback swamp and watched doves and emerald pigeons come in to water.

Much of the bush had a parklike feel to it, with little undergrowth, and the air there was moist, hot, soft. In mid-morning the verdure was strobed with tremulous light, and the entire world seemed to have gone green. Resting there against a termite mound, it was easy to see where the Boly-yases and Manu-manus came from.

One of the best of many good reasons to visit Seven Spirit Bay is for the fishing it offers, which can be as good as mixed-bag, light-tackle saltwater angling gets. Because the waters surrounding the lodge are part of a marine park and have never been commercially fished, the fishing is also as close to virgin as it is possible to find, with a profligate quantity and variety of gamefish.

The lodge is set up to provide three types of fishing, and it provides all three very well, with knowledgeable guides and good boats and equipment. For the less than fully committed angler, there are daily two- or three-hour trolls around the bay for trevallies, queenfish, and mackerel. Then there are half-day to full-day trips in the twenty-two-foot, 200-horse, aluminum center-console out to an inexhaustible supply of headlands, underwater reefs, and exposed rocks to cast with spinning tackle or medium-heavyweight fly gear for giant and gold trevallies, jacks, mackerel, and queen-fish—splendidly gamefish, all of them, ranging in size up to thirty or forty pounds. Patricia and I spent one morning happily at this with two young guides named Brett and Brett, hooking up frequently to big water-smashing, metallic-colored pelagic fish.

But the most interesting and unique fishing at Seven Spirit Bay is in Trepang Creek, a forty-five-minute bush drive from the lodge. One of numerous brackish-water creeks that rise inland on the peninsula and flow to the bay, we fished it, for a distance of maybe five miles from where the dinghies are kept to the mouth, casting flies and plugs into runoff gutters and arthritic-looking mangrove roots. The water was the color of coffee with one cream and full of deliberate life. Mud crabs clicked on the black mud banks; birds screeched and wheezed in the mangroves. And the creek, no wider in places than a back porch, snaked through unknowable vegetation to the sea.

In this small, slow, mysterious water we hooked baby tarpon, estuary cod, mangrove jacks, jack crevalle, queenfish, catfish, threadfin, and blue salmon, and the redoubtable barramundi. We boated many of these and released them all, as one is encouraged to do at Seven Spirit Bay. We also released, with riotous difficulty, a six-foot crocodile that our guide Brett hooked in the foot and had to bring to the boat to retrieve his plug. Once released, the crocodile hung in the water staring at us and feeling . . . what, exactly, it was hard to know, because he was going with his poker face.

At the estuary we lunched on a sandbar between the slides of two much larger crocodiles. Brett spread a tablecloth on the sand and we fed there on giant prawns and crawfish tails, mangoes, smoked salmon and mackerel, cubes of feta cheese, slices of ham, coleslaw with raisins, fruit, fresh rolls, and coconut cookies—a modest fishing lunch, perhaps, but enough to fortify us for the afternoon's hard work of angling our way back up Trepang Creek.

The days at Seven Spirit Bay tend to organize themselves gracefully and languidly between activities and comforts. You go to bed early there because there is very little else to do after dining and because the beds themselves are so inviting. And you wake early to rising bird sound and the knobby eucalyptus trees outside your habitat in intricate relief against a lemony sky. Watched by the wallaby family, scattering lizards, you walk over to the main building, to the groaning board of fresh fruits, juices, and cereals that is the breakfast buffet. One of the unfailingly cheerful waitresses brings you a plunger pot of coffee and you sit on the dining terrace in the cool, limp early air with whether or not to have a hot breakfast the only major decision on your plate.

Then you sail, or fish, or bush walk, and either have a brilliant lunch afield or return to the lodge for Thai beef, say, or scallops with a sweet dill vinaigrette. More wilderness interfacing activity in the afternoon (or a book by the pool and a nap), and then you ease into evening—ideally with a sundown swim and drink. I came very quickly to believe that the single best place on earth to have a gin and tonic was in the pool at Seven Spirit Bay with the sun sliding vividly into the sea. And I do not know of a nobler example of that drink than the one made there in a tall glass, by Michelle. Sipping from one of these, I would stroll around in the chest-deep water of the pool until dark, cooling and calming the day's ecological encountering both from within and without. Then a shower amid the ferns, and perhaps another drink at the bar—where Lena Horne sings from a CD at precisely the right volume—while you look over Chef Richard Harris's offerings for dinner.

"Cobourg Cuisine" is the tony description someone has hung on the cooking at Seven Spirit Bay, but they could call it roadkill and it would still be some of the best food I have ever eaten. The influences are well-chosen Indonesian, Thai, and Malayan; the ingredients of same-day-fresh local seafoods, tropical fruit and vegetables, and the best of Australia's very good meats, are unimprovable; and the preparation and presentation of the food are simply sensational. Every night the menu sings to you of appetizers such as Oven-Roasted Spatchcock Served with a Curried Tomato Relish; or Tempura Prawns with a Sweet Chili Lime-Leaf Dipping Sauce; or, for your main course, Char-Broiled Port Tenderloin Marinated in Rosemary, Honey, and Soy, Served with a Red Onion Marmalade, or Arafura Sea Bugs Sauteed with Vietnamese Hot Mint and Green Curry; and finally of Pecan Nut Butter Cake with Cinnamon Cream, Oranges Grand Marnier with Macadamia Nut Praline. . . . All this naming calling up delicacies that Warramurrungundji herself might be tempted to return for.

After only two or three days of this schedule at Seven Spirit Bay, I began to hear a sort of hum, one I have heard before but not often enough. It is the sound of deep luxury. Everywhere, of course, luxury is in the details. At Seven Spirit Bay it is in the linen kimonos, flashlights, and umbrellas provided you in your room for trips to the bath; in the butter rolled into little logs; in how there is never a leaf in the pool and how the napkins are folded; in how the staff caters to whatever you want before you know you want it. Deep luxury is having exactly what you need of these details in a given place—no more, no less. It is a matter of means being precisely sufficient to their ends, of luxury so natural to its environment and timed so perfectly that its production is invisible. Wherever you are lucky enough to find it, deep luxury just seems to ride the air and fall over you as diffusely as sunlight. Its only manifestations can sometimes be the simple happiness it stirs in you and the desperately dangerous sense that this is what life is *supposed* to be like; that and, for me at least, a faint reassuring hum it has to it, like a vacuum cleaner in a far-off room.

In this time when too many resort managers seem to think that luxury resides in how many swans or gondolas they can fit into the cascading pool, deep luxury is as rare as the rainbow pitta bird Patricia and I kept looking for in the bush at Seven Spirit Bay. It is a Doric column in an Ionic age, but it can still be found at some places, and Seven Spirit Bay is one of them.

On the evening before we left, I took a mountain bike ride out to the spectacular ocean overlook called Gunner's Quoin and came back to the lodge hot, muddy, and thirsty. Michelle made me a gin and tonic in the bar and I sat there with it, pecking at the mixed nuts and evidently looking hungry. Michelle disappeared into the kitchen and in a few minutes emerged with a heartbreakingly beautiful tray of golden trevally sashimi. She put this marvel down in front of me with a smile and offered me a pair of ornately carved chopsticks—a means precisely sufficient to an end. I finished the sashimi and carried my drink outside and into the pool. As I lolled and soaked there to an orange sunset, Michelle leaned over the terrace railing to ask me if there was anything else I required. "No thanks," I told her. Then I remembered that we were leaving the next day and realized in a small panic that a bus might run over me before I could land again in the lap of deep luxury.

I decided to try and sing up one last particular. "Michelle, there is one thing. Do you suppose tonight, as a sort of pre-appetizer appetizer, before the Grilled Scallops on the Salsa Salad, Patricia and I might have . . ."

"Another tray of sashimi?" she asked and, without waiting for an answer, said, "Consider it done."

14

MESSING ABOUT IN BOATS

There is nothing—absolutely nothing—half so much worth doing as simply messing about in boats.

—Water Rat, *The Wind in the Willows*

Amen to that, Rat!

And here we were again, my friend Jimbo Meador and I, two
long-standing disciples of the Water Rat, this time in a sixteen-
foot, sand-colored tandem kayak designed for precisely the kind of
messing about we were hard at. I sat in the bow, holding an eight-
weight fly rod, while Jimbo stood in the stern and poled us out of
the main channel into one of the countless little bays of the Louisiana marsh that are too muddy to wade and too shallow to enter
in anything other than what we were in.

At the rear of this bay, the wake of a cruising redfish swaggered
along just off the bank, and the kayak moved silently as a thought
over four inches of water toward an intersection with it. Jacked up
on the pure aboriginal exhilaration of bringing exactly the right
tool to a job, I began to sing to myself (oddly, you might think; so
did I) some of the words to W. S. Gilbert's lovesick water-rat song:
"For she is such a smart little craft, such a neat little, sweet little

craft—such a bright little, tight little, slight little, light little, trim little, slim little craft . . ."

"You might oughta cast," interjected Jimbo, because I was now close enough to the redfish to touch it with my rod and mesmerized by that fact—simply in love with how close to this still unconcerned fish our sweet little, trim little craft had brought us—I flipped out the fly and the redfish charged and ate it. Then he ran out to the middle of the bay and came unhooked. Jimbo and I looked at each other, grinning like . . . well, like Forrest Gump. And why not? As good as it gets had just gotten better.

It is said that during the media furor created by the release of the movie version of a novel written by his lifelong friend Winston Groom, Jimbo was asked in an interview with a *New York Times* writer if it were true that he was the real-life inspiration for the character Forrest Gump. "I guess," Jimbo replied, then added after a pause: "All but the idiot part."

What makes that line particularly funny to his countless friends is that no one we know has led a less idiotic life than Jimbo. A man about whom it is impossible to find anyone to say anything even slightly disparaging, he owns a Sufi elder's fortune of kind and generous imperturbability, amassed over a lifetime of following his bliss as implacably and enthusiastically as a beagle on a rabbit scent. Jimbo's bliss has been his freedom, and that freedom has always been found on the water and in boats. His first was a fourteen-foot, cross-planked cypress rowboat, given to him by his father when he was seven or eight. The family lived in Mobile and, in the summers, across the bay in Fairhope, where Jimbo still lives. There was a black man named Duke Cox who did odd jobs for them, and he and Jimbo would take the rowboat into Mobile Bay to seine shrimp and catch speckled trout with Calcutta cane

poles and popping corks to sell to the fish market in Fairhope.
When he was fifteen, he graduated to a Stauter-built skiff with a
15-horse Evinrude, and to plug fishing and dragging a shrimp
trawl; then later to live-bait fishing in the Gulf in an eighteen-and-
a-half-foot deep-V Negus.

After discovering that college wasn't wet enough, Jimbo
worked on a tugboat all over the Gulf Coast, for a stevedoring
company, on a bay shrimper, and as manager of a seafood process-
ing plant. When that last job got too office oriented, he bought a
Hewes skiff and started guiding recreational fishermen in Mobile
Bay and repping for Hewes. Giving fly-casting lessons for the Orvis Company led next to a job as Orvis's Southeast business manager, and when that turned into driving more cars than boats, he
became director of sales for another flatboat company, Hell's Bay
Boatworks.

While working for Orvis and later Hell's Bay, Jimbo spent a lot
of time fishing the Louisiana marsh and being given the fin by
redfish and specs up in bays and creeks too shallow for even the

lightest of skiffs. By this time he had owned dozens of boats, from skiffs and canoes to deep-Vs and sailboats, and had become a student of the subject. After some pondering, it seemed to him that a kayak was the answer to his problem, but he knew of none on the market that was designed for fishing. Then, at an outdoor retailers show in the mid-1990s, he met Andy Zimmerman, at that time the owner of Wilderness Systems Kayaks, who, as it happened, had been working on a prototype angling kayak. Andy sent one of them to Jimbo, who began fishing from it in the Gulf marshes (possibly the first person to do so since the Indians) and immediately loved everything about it: its simplicity and long history with the native peoples; the exercise, solitude, and silence it afforded; the way it allowed him to become an integral part of the marsh, subject to its winds and currents, rather than an engined intruder; and, not least, the access it provided to otherwise inaccessible fishing.

The more Jimbo fished from the Wilderness Systems' kayak, the more ways he saw to improve its design. Not long after their original meeting, Andy Zimmerman sold Wilderness Systems and signed a five-year noncompete agreement. During that period he and Jimbo traded ideas about what the perfect fishing kayak would be, and when Andy's noncompete period was over he decided to start a new company to build it.

That company, Legacy Paddlesports, now turns out over a hundred fishing kayaks a day, ranging in size from a nine-and-a-half-foot, thirty-eight-pound Featherlite to a seventy-eight-pound, sixteen-foot tandem. Built of a light and durable superlinear polyethylene, the little boats conflate a decade of Jimbo's and Andy's design ideas: a patented tunnel hull that allows for enough stability to stand up and fish, surprisingly comfortable seats and footrests, clips for rod holders, a groove in the bow to lay your rod tip in, and a sliding anchor-trolley system. All this makes for a sort of clawhammer of a boat—something designed to do one thing just about as well as it can be done—and I am here to tell you that the only possible response to being in it when it does it is to grin like Forrest Gump.

"That looked like a Robart hook set," shouted Gary Taylor from his skiff at the mouth of the bay where he and photographer Squire Fox had watched me lose my fish. Robart is the name of an angling-challenged mutual friend of mine and Gary's. I wondered if Robart was often singing little ditties to himself when it came time to cast or strike a fish, and determined to dislocate the jaw of the next redfish to eat my fly.

An ex-motorcycle racer, welder, professional bass fisherman, and Louisiana mosquito-control director, Gary Taylor is now one of the best redfish-specializing guides on the Gulf Coast. Almost all of his guiding is done in what is known as the Louisiana marsh, if you happen to be from Louisiana, or the Biloxi marsh if you are from Mississippi. By either name it is a 650-square-mile maze of unpeopled grassy islands, oyster bars, channels and bays, some sixteen miles offshore of Gary's hometown of Slidell, Louisiana, and it offers up what is likely the finest shallow-water redfishing in the country. Despite that fact, you rarely, if ever, see another recreational fishing boat in the marsh, and that is because of both its distance from shore and the serious dues that have to be paid to learn where its fish are, to fish it effectively, and even to keep from getting lost in it. Gary has paid those dues for over two decades and no one knows the marsh better. Moreover, he has found an ingenious solution to the problem of needing both a good-size seaworthy boat to cross the often-rough Lake Borgne between Slidell and the marsh, and a poleable, shallow-draft skiff to fish from once he is there. That solution is the *Mr. Champ*, a 210-

diesel, thirty-one-foot Lafitte skiff, rigged with an electric winch and cradle to carry a skiff on its deck. As Gary is one of the growing number of guides whom Jimbo has sold on the glories of the kayak, it is also rigged to carry three of those on the wheel-house roof.

With all these moving parts and various crafts to mess about in, a fishing day is neither easy nor short for Gary Taylor. Typically it begins at 4 a.m. and ends after dark, with a run across Lake Borgne of between forty-five minutes and two hours each way, depending on where in the marsh he is going, and it is filled with more manual labor than most guides do in a week. Also, because the marsh lies in unprotected water, there is often too much wind to fish it at all. What makes the effort and chanciness more than worth it to Gary and his clients are those days when there is little or no wind, and sun enough to spot the fish: days like the one Jimbo and I and our friend Tom Montgomery had had a few years before—in January when the big Gulf reds are in the marsh.

We began fishing around ten thirty on that sunny, windless day, Jimbo poling and casting from the platform of his skiff, and Tom and I with Gary in his. After a five-minute run from where we had anchored and left the *Mr. Champ*, we were covered up in big redfish cruising along the edge of a bank. Jimbo staked out at the bottom end of the bank and caught four without moving. I blew the first fish I threw to, then caught a twenty-four pounder and then another almost as big. There were fish all around the boat, so Gary came down off the platform and he and I doubled up. Then I gave the fly rod to Tom and he caught one, then a second, dou-bling up again with Gary. Before lunchtime, we had caught sixteen redfish between fifteen and twenty-five pounds. The fishing stayed hot until around two when we left fish to find fish (some-thing even your Labrador retriever knows not to do). And it was hot again for most of the three or four hours we fished the next day, an overcast one, going to blind-casting spinning rods in the bad light and catching eight or nine more reds up to twenty-two pounds.

We were overnighting in the marsh on that trip, and when we came back to the *Mr. Champ* after fishing on the first day, Jimbo and Gary "cooned" some oysters off a bar, then culled and shucked them on the back deck while I filleted the only redfish under ten pounds we had caught and opened a Pinot Grigio. We sucked some of the oysters out of the shells and added the rest to a gumbo Gary's wife had made that was heating on a Coleman stove. Gary grilled the redfish fillets "on the half shell," scales and skin down, and we ate them with the gumbo, rice, and salad, and drank more wine and sat on the deck watching the gulls and terns and white pelicans, listening to a light breeze off the Gulf and talking.

Tom, with more days of angling under his belt and on his passport than anyone I know, said the fishing we had had that day was as good as it gets, and no one was going to argue with him.

"Yeah, but pretty soon," said Jimbo, "I'm gonna have a surprise for y'all that's gonna make it even better."

And so it was, I thought, even as my second redfish came unstuck from the fly, this one after a five-minute fight, and my hook set was again compared by Gary to Robart's. After all, it was only ten o'clock, on a beautiful April morning of workable wind and sun. Sure it was a little unusual to have two fish in a row come unhooked, and more than a little inconvenient for Squire who was trying to get a picture of one, and for Gary who was poling his ass off behind our kayak to help Squire do that. But there were plenty of fish around, they were eating, and Jimbo was poling the kayak up close enough to net them. The black dog who often accompanies me on the water would surely go home for lunch, I told myself: I couldn't possibly lose a third fish.

But the dog didn't, and I did. And then a fourth, a fifth, and a *sixth*, before finally bringing in a seven pounder for Squire's long-awaited photograph.

A few years ago, Tom and I were fishing with two guides in the Everglades and had camped out for the night in one of those little huts on stilts they have down there. After dinner one of the guides lit an expensive kerosene lantern as we sat on the deck of the hut chatting and smoking cigars. After a while I stood up to get something and accidentally knocked the lantern over and broke it. The guide looked at the shattered glass a bit wistfully, said the obligatory things about how it wasn't my fault, and lit the other one he had brought. A half hour later I got up for something else and *broke it too*. At that point there was only silence. I went to bed. The next morning Tom told me the three of them had sat in the dark for a full ten minutes before the guide who had owned the lanterns finally broke the silence. "Jesus," he said, "it's like the guy was on a *mission*."

Gary's jibes and Jimbo's soothing not-your-faults gave way after the fourth or fifth lost fish to that same stunned "how is this fucking *possible*?" silence. I don't think any of us had ever seen anything like it. If I knew how to repeat it, I could probably get rich doing it as a magician's act.

And I couldn't have cared less. At another time it might have made me try to swim back home. But on that day, as we ghosted along in that idea of a boat become a perfected reality into virgin channels and bays, watching mullet jump and swallows and red-wing blackbirds sortie-ing above the tan grass, I felt not a twinge of appropriate embarrassment, only a growing elation—a sort of Zenned-out journey-not-the-destination well-being in simply moving as naturally as an alligator through that blessedly pristine place, with no noise marking our passage, and the bending of the fly rod through its lovely arc like wind bending the grass. If the fish wanted to spit out my hooks till kingdom come—*Hey*?

Such was my euphoria over the magic of kayak fishing that as far as I was concerned the black dog could have quit swimming behind us and just ridden around with Jimbo and me enjoying the marsh. But he did go home that afternoon, when Jimbo and I caught plenty of fish from separate kayaks. And he stayed at home the next day when Gary also got into a kayak and the three of us— each in his own neat little craft—took some rods and went messing about again in boats.

15

IF YOU BUILD IT THEY WILL COME (AND FISH!)

One of the notable things that makes the super-rich different from maybe you and certainly me is that the possession of resources far beyond any conceivable physical need often acts on them like a sort of hallucinogen. They tend to walk around with visions in the lizard portion of their brain, having two important advantages where those visions are concerned over those of us who might have retched over a peyote bud or two or dropped a tab of acid here and there: They can better insulate themselves against those visions they find unpalatable, and they can actualize even the most far-fetched of the ones that appeal to them.

Say you are just sitting around one day, a young Chilean banker with a tooth for fishing and adventure, and into your head floats the vision of a very big boat carrying a helicopter, a variety of smaller boats, and an overall tab way north of $20 million that will allow you to become the first person on the planet to fully and luxuriously access the wilderness paradise of fishing and adventure whose doorway is Chile's Patagonian coastline. Most of us would just sleep it off, no?

"This is a vision that existed only in my head," said Andres Ergas. "Now, you can see it is real."

I *could* see that; and a bit surreal as well—very like something I might want an opium dream to be. There before us, tied fore and aft to a dock in the Chilean port town of Puerto Montt, was the gleaming, blue-hulled, five-decked *Atmosphere*, and standing in a smart line in front of it was its grinning and uniformed crew of thirty-two, who in a few moments would begin a six-day campaign of falling all over themselves to make me and my fifteen fellow passengers more comfortable and variously happy than we had any right to be.

In addition to the ship's captain (a Chilean naval officer with a rank just below admiral), two pilots, and the engine crew, there was an expedition manager, a helicopter pilot, four ecotour guides, three chefs, bartenders, waiters, maids, eight fishing guides, two fetching and efficient young ladies whose titles were "hostess" and "concierge," a masseuse . . . and, introducing us to all these people, there was our host—the well-heeled, energetic young visionary from whose head Nomads of the Seas: Patagonia by Air, Land and Water had sprung full-blown only three months before.

Andres Ergas turned forty while we were on his ship with him that week. On board to celebrate his birthday were some friends from Santiago, his wife and two young daughters, and his mother and father. The father, Jacob, had made a fortune in banking and other ventures in Santiago after moving there from Germany as a young man, only to have it all appropriated, along with his house and lands by the Allende government when that government took office in 1970. Suddenly and thoroughly dispossessed, Jacob moved his young family to Brownsville, Texas. Starting with nothing in a foreign country, he made a second fortune there in banking, and then a third—the largest yet—when he moved the family back to Chile in 1978 after the Pinochet coup that put Allende out of power. Now one of Chile's best-known and most successful businessmen, with half interest in the country's second-largest bank, among other assets, Jacob is tall, gentle, exquisitely polite. But unmistakably, he is also an old lion who has snacked on a lot of rival's lunches, and a past master (and role model for his son) at making dreams snap to and happen with no questions asked.

Andres is bright and solidly built, with icy blue eyes and the three- or four-day stubble of beard that South American men seem to own from birth. He is an expert skier on snow and water, an experienced jetboat jockey, an ex-military sniper, and an officer in the Chilean Air Force Reserve who is licensed to fly both helicopters and fixed-wing planes: an adrenaline junkie, in short, for whom fifteen dutiful years in the banking business was rich soil for the growth of visions.

The Nomads of the Seas concept came to him during a three-week camping trip he made to a remote lake in Chilean Patagonia in 1997. Much of that part of the country—a narrow twenty-two-hundred-kilometer-long strip of magnificently wild and largely roadless landscape, bordered by the Pacific to the west, the Andes to the east, and the towns of Puerto Montt and Punta Arenas to the north and south—is inaccessible except by helicopter, float-plane, or live-aboard mother ship, and a large percentage of its myriad trout-holding rivers, lakes, and lagoons, and its countless estuaries with their seasonal runs of salmon, have never been fished. Taken as a whole, and in its potential, Chilean Patagonia is probably the greatest and most varied salmonid fishery on earth. With its fiords and bays, its snowcapped volcanoes, waterfalls, and rainforests towered over by the Andes, it is certainly one of the most stunningly beautiful places on earth; and with its prolific bird and marine life, from penguins and sea lions to blue and hump-backed whales, it is unquestionably one of the finest ecotourism destinations on earth.

And yet, mused Andres Ergas on his camping trip, practically no one can *get to* much of it. What if . . .

Custom-built in Chile, the *Atmosphere* is an expedition cruise ship with an overall length of 150 feet, a beam of 33 feet, a top speed of fourteen knots, and a range of six thousand nautical miles. To go comfortably and safely to any place Andres might want to take it, it is fitted out with state-of-the-art electronics, twin-screw propulsion, a steel hull, bow-thrusters, and stabilizers. In addition to its large crew, it accommodates up to twenty-eight passengers in fourteen well-appointed guest cabins, each with a sea view and private bathroom. It has an immaculate, all stainless steel Isselbaecher kitchen; a main salon, divided into bar, lounging, and dining areas, that is lavishly windowed and large enough for a game of touch football; a locker room for changing in and out of waders; four open-air saltwater hot tubs, a sauna, and a massage room.

But what distinguishes the *Atmosphere* from your run-of-the-mill small luxury cruise ship is the elaborate vision-delivery system of conveyances it carries aft of the salon. Back there, along with two eight-ton-capacity knuckle cranes to lift them in and out of the water, are six twenty-foot, 200-horsepower Rogue jetboats, four McKenzie-style driftboats, six inflatable Zodiacs, and a $250,000 sixteen-passenger, thirty-three-foot Zodiac Hurricane RIB with twin 250-horsepower four-stroke outboards and a top speed of fifty-five miles per hour. A heliport above all those water toys is residence to a cherry-red, six-passenger Bell 407 helicopter—the air component of the "air, land and water" raids that Nomads of the Seas now makes weekly from October through the first week of May on the pristine piscatorial riches of the southern Chilean coastline.

Given that Andres, his captain, his chopper pilot, and his expedition manager are all military men, it is perhaps unsurprising that a week aboard the *Atmosphere* has more than a few martial resonances, albeit ones that are well-poached in luxury. You can bounce a dime off the beds in your stateroom, which are made twice a day. You are required to remove your shoes before entering the salon. Everything from meals to the vast logistics of daily fishing and ecotouring up to twenty-eight top-dollar, and thus demanding, guests is done on time and almost without error. Even the language of the ship's potential destinations in a given week has a campaign color to it: Five different "zones of penetration" south of Puerto Montt, each with four separate anchorages, and each anchorage with eighteen locations where trout and salmon can be engaged by the Nomads' troops.

All this to catch a *fish*, you might wonder? Well, yes and no. It is perfectly possible to spend an idyllic week on the *Atmosphere* eating the splendid food, hot-tubbing and being massaged, venturing out occasionally in the big Zodiac with its crew of four eager young ecoguides to watch all manner of birdlife, sea lions, penguins, and whales; and, in the evenings, listening to the marine-ecology lectures given by those guides, and watching the after-dinner slide show of the day's events, prepared by them and the fishing guides—all while developing an intimacy with the ship's copious store of good Chilean wines.

However, it is also possible to be my friend Tom Rosenbauer and quite enjoy yourself. Rosenbauer, who put together the group of journalists of which I was a part on board the ship, is marketing director of fly fishing for the Orvis Company and an expert, rabid, and insatiable trout angler who never drew a nonfishing breath all week. On a hopelessly rainy day (and they are not uncommon in Chilean Patagonia), when it appeared the helicopter might not fly, he chose to wait on the ship in the hope that it would, instead of going whale watching with the rest of our group. The weather cleared. In the big Zodiac we had humpbacked and ninety-foot blue whales breaching, spouting, and fluking close around us all day long—a glorious, thrilling, once-in-a-lifetime show. Rosenbauer had a thirty-fish day. Everyone was happy.

Nomads of the Seas advertises its angling program as "extreme fly fishing," which is both misleading and apt. Though some of the wading might require a reasonable degree of fitness, there is nothing arduous about the fishing; nor is it technically very difficult; nor is there any "you fall, you die" extreme-skiing sort of jeopardy attached to it. It is, however, sublimely extreme in the sense that you are casting flies in serious wilderness to fish that may never have seen one before; and, God knows, the effort and money and transportation ingenuity required to put you in position to make those casts are nothing if not extreme.

On a typical week's trip, the *Atmosphere* will stop in three or four anchorages, from thirty to three hundred miles south of Puerto Montt. The ship travels at night, and one of the uniquely exhilarating experiences it affords is to wake at dawn, carry a cup of coffee up to the wheelhouse deck, and find yourself in some ravishing new bay or fiord with the snowy top of a volcano catching first light above the rainforested hillsides and porpoises rolling around the boat.

After breakfast, you, a guide, and another angler are helicoptered or jetboated to your fishing location for the day. It could be a lake or a lagoon, where waiting for you is one of the thirty driftboats that Andres has choppered in to various locations and left there; or a river that you will float in one of the inflatable Zodiacs. Or you might have chosen to experiment for the day at one of the many estuaries into which, from November through March, enter runs of native coho and king salmon, as well as some Atlantic salmon and steelhead fish-farm escapees. In truth, Nomads did not yet, when we were there, have a proper handle on the estuarial fishery, but Andres plans to find one and its potential for future clients is enormous.

In the meantime, the inland fishery for rainbow, brown, and brook trout can be sufficiently varied and productive to satisfy even the most demanding angler, and it will only improve as Andres and his guides discover more virgin trout waters on their frequent scouting trips. A number of people in our group had days when they lost count of the fish they released. And though none of the leviathan trout of ten pounds or more that Chile regularly offers up were caught in our week, plenty in the four- to six-pound range were.

My favorite day was one I spent with my pal Tom Montgomery, Andres, and his expedition manager, Osvaldo. A formidably tough and resourceful ex–Special Forces officer in the Chilean army and chief bodyguard to Pinochet when he was president of Chile, Osvaldo is also—as is Andres—a charming and merry man who can take as unfettered and pure a pleasure in a day of fishing as any boy on a catfish creek. From a particularly lovely anchorage in Tic Toc Bay, we rode a jetboat up a large, milky glacial river, with Andres slewing enthusiastically through rapids and around logs at thirty miles per hour, then up a clear, smaller river to its mouth at a startlingly beautiful lake of white sand beaches and many islands, with an enormous glacier rearing above it to the east and the Andean Cordillera to the west—the very lake on which Andres had camped in 1997.

It was a calm, warm day, and above the great amphitheater of the lake, condors floated on thermals against an infinitely blue sky. We took turns fishing a reed bed at the far end of the lake, both from the boat and wading, and it was the very finest kind of fishing—relaxed, conversational, as bright as the day with good humor and spirit. The trout, mostly rainbows, were feeding on dragonflies, sometimes jumping all the way out of the water to take one, and we caught many of them between sixteen and twenty-two inches on big dry flies. Out of a long lifetime of wetting fly lines, I cannot recall a more enjoyable morning of doing so, or a more handsome place to do it.

After more easygoing fishing in the afternoon, we would finish off the day with some up-close dolphin and whale sightings in Tic Toc Bay and a visit to a rock island carpeted with sea lions, who stared at us with great romantic eyes, their boxer's ears cocked, and then—to whoops of Osvaldo's laughter—flippered goofily off the island to frolic around the boat. Then it was on to a hot tub and massage, and a dinner that started with little cups of ceviche, followed by octopus sashimi and perfectly cooked rabbit tenderloin with polenta and wild mushrooms.

But before all that we met up for lunch with my nephew, Monte Burke, and his boat mate and their guide, who had been fishing the river flowing out of the lake from another jetboat with results as good as ours.

At the same lakeshore campsite that Andres had used as a base for his first exploration of the area in 1997, we cracked a bottle or two of *vino tinto* while Osvaldo and the guide built a fire for a Chilean *asado* of beef and sausages. On the lake a black-necked swan was in full, stately cruise, its backdrop a green cliff down which dropped the bright thread of a two hundred-foot waterfall. If life was a bone, this would be some of the meat closest to it, and I told Andres that as we loafed after lunch with Partagas stogies and satisfied minds. Then I asked him if his old campsite might be conjuring up for him any new visions.

"My aim is in ten years," he said, "to have three ships doing what we do now—one based in Puerto Montt, one in Punta Arenas, and one in between. The whole Patagonian coastline . . . *imagine* it, Charles!

It was a nice invitation, but with my bank account I would have to have been smoking something other than a cigar.

16

WHAT A PLACE TO WET A LION

The members of some Zambezi River tribes, I had been told the day before, believe that crocodiles are their reincarnated ancestors, and that the shocking percentage of themselves that meet their Maker every year via crocodile are individuals who were unkind to their parents. I was brought to a disconcerting recollection of these beliefs by Roelof as soon as I stepped out of the boat onto the jungly shore and took my first cast with a big streamer fly into the murky roil of the Zambezi.

"I'd move a good meter away from the bank, if I were you," he said and smiled. "That way you might at least see the croc before it takes you."

Being backed up to thorn trees while trying to remember every insult visited on my long-suffering father during my adolescence did nothing for my backcast, and as I fished my wide-eyed way down the bank, I was struck with a disturbing irony: I was, after all, here largely because of my father. . . . Could this be a setup?

Who other than he—an insatiable and world-traveled angler— was responsible for my having eccentrically mooned away my youth over outdoor magazines with dreams of the barramundi and black marlin of Australia, the noble mahseer of India, the dorado of northern Argentina, the fearsome tigerfish of the Zambezi? Now, having pursued those dreams as immoderately as a crack addict for over forty years, the tigerfish and mahseer were the last ones uncaught from my boyhood wish list. Here I was, finally angling for one of them, botching every cast in a cold sweat of Iron Age magical thinking and feeling ripe for reprisal.

Ridiculous, you say; but were there not omens? Like the dead and rotting eight-pound tigerfish Roelof had found floating in the river that now lay where he had placed it on the bank, seeming to grin at me around its preposterous dentures; or the pair of baboons twenty meters off under a thorn tree who watched me like blood-sport fans, cackling and scratching their asses; or the submerged hippos cruising by with their periscope eyes alight with anticipation. And when the growing dark finally put an end to my timorous and fishless casting, it was with relief that I retired to the boat with Roelof, my irrepressibly cheerful young friend Teddy Grennan and photographer Hakan Stenlund.

Grilled chicken wings and restorative gin and tonics in hand, we watched a giant blood-orange sun set behind a tableau of wading elephants. "What a place to wet a lion," commented Teddy, then broke into his sorely off-key version of "The Lion Sleeps Tonight," which was to score our entire stay in Zambia. The wretched pun and song somehow bucked me up, and as the boat carried us back upriver in the cooling air toward the camp, I had all but come around when an enormous crocodile crashed into the water from the bank not ten meters away.

"Twelve or fifteen feet," said Roelof. "Magnificent creatures. They have no predators, you know. A croc that big would be close to fifty years old."

About the same age as my father when I was making his life a living hell.

Roelof Schutte and his pretty wife, Helen, manage Old Mondoro, one of six safari camps in Zambia's 4,082-square-kilometer Lower Zambezi National Park. The park was opened in 1983 and has since become, through steady and rigorous conservation efforts, one of the top game-viewing parks in Africa, as well as one of the world's premier destinations for tigerfish angling. The best months for that angling, September and October, are Zambia's hottest and driest months. At that time the 120 kilometers of the Zambezi River inside the park are both a magnet and a haven for animals, and their density in and around the river is nothing short of staggering. There are over seventy hippos for example, to every half mile of river. Day and night they wander near and through the camp, along with elephants, baboons, and African buffalo. Over the next five days at Old Mondoro and its sister camp, Sausage Tree, I could have dropped dozens of flies onto the noses of all of those animals, as well as crocodiles and waterbucks, with no cast longer than twenty meters away. I might even have hooked one of them on a *backcast*.

It is this abundance of proximate wildlife that gives the angling on the Lower Zambezi the surreal, Disneyesque coloration that everyone who has ever fished there mentions. It also has the dangerous tendency of making you feel you are in a "park" park—a harmless, Americanized sort of place where the thing over there on the trail to your tent is really a kid named Ralph from Iowa City who is working his way through college by wearing a buffalo get-up.

"You don't go anywhere after dark without one of the staff accompanying you," Roelof told us at dinner. "During the day you are free to walk around on your own, but keep your eyes open and

if you see an elephant or hippo or buffalo between you and where you are going, come and get someone. *Don't* walk up to it."

We were sitting around a fire with Roelof and Helen and a nice couple from London, cigars and port putting the finishing touches to a splendid feed of Zambezi bream taken at a table set outside with linen and crystal, and lit, as were the bar and dining pavilion, by kerosene lanterns. Old Mondoro is the smallest (a maximum of eight guests) of the lodges in the park and less elaborate than some, but Teddy, Hakan, and I were finding it perfectly to our tastes. My spirits had lifted considerably, as they generally do to the ministrations of good food and alcohol, and as I listened to the huffing of hippos from the river and other unidentified coughs and sighings coming from the winter thorn jungle surrounding us, it seemed clear that my earlier fearful funk had been the product of a sullen, self-involved Camusian estrangement. All I needed to do to catch fish and enjoy myself in this wonderland of God's creatures, I decided, was to relax and become one with it.

I had a chance to try out that approach as soon as I was led back to my riverside sleeping chalet—a wonderfully comfortable affair, by the way, made of reed, thatch, and canvas, with an open-air bathroom—when the flashlight held by the young man accompanying me picked up a hippo standing just five feet off the path. This, I was told, was Norman, a young bull who disliked fighting, was fond of Helen, and was a frequent visitor to the camp. Wearing a becoming wreath of water hyacinth around his considerable neck, Norman contentedly munched thorn tree pods as I watched him for four or five minutes. Hippos are said to be responsible for killing more people every year than any animal in Africa, but there was clearly no murderous intent here; and because I admired his hyacinth garland (worn perhaps for Helen?) and have always been more a lover than a fighter myself, I had no trouble at all becoming one with Norman before toddling off to bed.

Hakan, Teddy, and I had a sunrise breakfast at five fifteen the next morning with Roelof, and by then I had already become one with a white frog, a silver lizard, and a garrulous, long-beaked bird in my chalet, and with hundreds of laughing doves in the trees around the eating pavilion whose cooings were our breakfast iPod track. But all that wasn't even an appetizer for the smorgasbord of at-oneness opportunities we encountered over the next three and a half hours on a walking safari with Roelof, an AK-47-armed park warden, and the couple from London.

Roelof's opening safety lecture ("Don't run unless you are told to. If I tell you to get behind a tree or a termite mound, please do it *now*. Don't take pictures of a charging animal") struck me as a bit obligatory and overblown as we stood listening to it on the riverbank, which this morning seemed nothing less than a Peaceable Kingdom of plover and Egyptian geese, exquisite white-fronted bee-eaters, a troop of chattering monkeys, and a raft of hippos lying submerged in the river like speed bumps with eyes. As we walked, Roelof pointed out various animal tracks, bird nests, lion-ant hills, and gave us a fifteen-minute treatise on the sociology and architectural intricacies of a ten-foot termite mound which, though impassioned, left me incompletely connected to those insects.

A sexy, no-nonsense little female warthog was easier. She pranced up very close to our group and stared at us with attitude, her feisty face, curly mane, and pretty haunches reminiscent somehow of Britney Spears. I had no problem feeling at one with her; nor with four old buffalo bulls lying in a grassy opening who had a grumpy, early-morning look of various joints paining them with which I am too familiar; nor with the herds of skittish impala, the troops of curious baboons, the great white-bibbed fish eagle eyeing the river for breakfast from the top of a tree. As we wandered quietly in single-file among the well-spaced thorn trees, through shafts of candied morning light, learning why hyena dung is white and how to tell the shoulder height of an elephant by its track, I fancied I could feel myself emerging from my twenty-first-century cocoon of natural estrangement into a fine, primordial empathy. "*Yes,*" I would have shouted to the animals but for Roelof's certain disapproval: "I *feel* your alertness, your curiosity, your fears, your appetites . . ."

It was with appetite in particular that I found my strongest empathy toward the end of the long walk when we sat on a termite mound and watched a big bull elephant *à table*, as I was hoping soon to be, gorging himself on thorn tree pods, grass, and anything else that came to trunk. Either indifferent to or unaware of our presence, he fed up to within thirty feet of us and was moving closer when the warden knocked loudly on the stock of his rifle, interrupting the old chap's meal and sending him off in an understandable huff.

Partially, perhaps, out of a desire to make up for the warden's rudeness, and partially because of my new empathetic expansiveness, I was led shortly after lunch into nearly getting mud holes stomped into Teddy and myself. On our way back to the chalets for a nap we spied three elephants, very close to Teddy's chalet, drinking out of the river. One of them, a young bull, was missing a tusk and was acting chesty with the other two out of an obvious tusk envy, which, after we had observed it for a while, seemed to me something I might be able to work with. I strolled down closer to the elephants, Teddy following with his video camera going, and then closer—at which point all three turned around to look at us.

"Where do you think their comfort zone stops?" asked Teddy, referring to the invisible line of proximity to elephants that Roelof had warned us not to cross, without specifying where exactly it was.

"I'd say about here," I allowed, noticing a distinct change of demeanor in One-Tusk. I was on the point of sharing with him how I myself was missing a big toe, when he and the other two began trotting uphill toward us, their ears raised. Teddy and I backed up, then turned and ran, with the elephants hot on our heels. We burst into Teddy's chalet only feet ahead of One-Tusk, who waved his trunk and eyed us malignantly, his great wagging ear filling the open door.

"He could, you know, knock this little building down with ..." I turned to Teddy who was grinning and filming with his video camera.

"Could you put your face between the camera and that guy's head?" he asked me. "Your expression is priceless." But I was already around him, headed for the back wall of the chalet which was open above waist height . . . and filled with the looming bulk of another elephant.

"Quick, the bathroom!" I said and scurried for it, planning to jump its enclosing wall, but there guarding it stood the third beast. Feeling doomed, I turned around. We were surrounded by ten tons of irked elephants in a tiny thatch hut, and Teddy, whose empathy must extend nobly beyond my own, was filming and saying, "Could you just reach your hand out like you're going to pat him?"

I would love to tell you that, properly chastened by One-Tusk and his friends into an attitude of respectful humility before the great natural world, I went on upriver to Sausage Tree camp after our near Grizzly Man experience and fished as instinctively and productively as a fish eagle, filling up the boat with the tigerfish of my boyhood dreams. Alas, I cannot.

What I can tell you is that the camp itself, for all its remoteness, is a marvel of creature comforts. You sleep on a sumptuous bed in a spacious Bedouin-style tent made of reed and white canvas, under linen sheets and a down duvet. Power for lights and fans, and the hot water for your shower, is provided by a silenced generator. Your meals are cheffed by Honore, trained in Paris, and taken on a platform hanging dramatically above the river in the shade of a sausage tree. And your every wish—for a fresh towel by the pool? for another of the addictive Brian's Specials from the eponymous bartender?—is attended to, almost before it can be uttered, by your own personal tent valet, or by the charming young managers, Dave and Tash Dower.

Moreover, the camp's owners, Allan Harkness and Jason Mott—who also own half interest in Old Mondoro—have judiciously kept all the emollients in perfect harmony with the place and the experience it offers, avoiding the cloying ultra-luxury of some of the $1,000 a day African "camps." Pampered as you are, Sausage Tree is much more about what you do there than what is done for you. And there is no shortage of things to occupy your time, all centered as they should be on the astounding wildlife of the park. Every day you may choose among a variety of ways to observe that wildlife: safaris by foot, boat, or vehicle, and a truly stunning four-hour canoe trip down the lovely Chifungulu Channel, during which you paddle carefully around God's own amount of hippos and crocs while trying to take in the clouds of ibis, egrets, Goliath herons, and other birds, the loafing elephants and buffalo, the bounding impala and waterbuck. My own favorite activities were the night game drives. The most vivid moments of our trip for me were sitting with a predinner gin and tonic in the back of a slow-moving safari vehicle under the leaning equatorial stars, breathing in the ineffably sweet and nostalgic odor of a freshly fallen night by water and watching nocturnal animals ghost in and out of the torch held by our guide: a spaniel-size honey badger with a smart white stripe down his back who grunted as he walked; two groups of lions, one composed of three harried-looking females and seven or eight cubs who play-stalked our vehicle.

And then, of course, there is the fishing (an official and guided activity at Sausage Tree, a do-it-yourself one at Old Mondoro). Most of it is done, often quite productively, with heavy spinning rods and hooks baited with chicken hearts. If you want to sport for the tigers with fly rods, fine, and you can catch them that way, but you are laying yourself open to the vagaries that always attend refined technique. Such as fish who bite at, but won't eat, a fly.

Believe me, that was the last thing I had expected from *Hydrocynus vittalus*, the "striped river dog," who is a relative of the piranha, grows to over thirty pounds in the Zambezi, and is legendary for his ferocious aggressiveness. But Hakan, Teddy, and I found them to be as coy as debutantes in their eating habits.

With the hardworking Charles as our guide, we spent hour after blistering hour (the temperature reached 120 Fahrenheit while we were there) pounding the banks from a safari boat with all manner of streamers and poppers, drawing frequent and maddening swirls at the flies and short-takes, but precious few eats. Finally, on the second day, Hakan broke through with a fat nine pounder that jumped and ran impressively and was then photographed and admired for the awesome piece of work it was: a silver chassis with black stripes, an orange-and-black tail, and a face full of outsized fangs that looked like it was purchased in the Halloween section of Walmart. Then Teddy, a rank long-rod amateur, caught a small one to yet another chorus of "The Lion Sleeps Tonight." Hakan caught a small one and lost a larger one. Teddy caught *another* small one . . . and I began to sour.

I like to think I am long past being competitive about fishing, but this seemed unfair. All I wanted was one good fish (perhaps a tad bigger than Hakan's)—to catch it cleanly; hold and study it for a moment, using the expensive BogaGrip gadget I had bought for lifting toothy fish without losing a finger; and release it unharmed, as a token set free from an old dream. Oh, and to get a photo of it to hang on my wall.

But by the second afternoon at Sausage Tree that simple wish had begun to seem cruelly unattainable. I had given my rod to Teddy and was sitting in a snit with a beer, watching all the hippos and things on the bank who now seemed nothing more than pain-in-the-ass impediments to catching my fish. Bitterly, I asked Teddy and Hakan if they knew of another place in the world where, while peacefully angling, you could have your boat turned over by a hippo, lose a leg to a croc as you swam for shore, then, once you had made it, be stomped by an elephant, gored by a buffalo, and have what was left of you eaten by lions. So much for empathy.

They both looked at me pityingly.

"Why don't you take a few casts?" said Teddy, and handed me my rod. "I'm worn out from catching these things."

I tied on the biggest, ugliest popper I had, grimly took the bow, cast . . . and hooked my fish! It jumped gloriously (showing itself to be maybe a tad bigger than Hakan's), and everything for a few brief moments was right again with the world. But after Charles had BogaGripped the fish and stuck his hand up through its gills to remove the fly, it began to gush blood. I took the BogaGrip from Charles, both to weigh the fish and to hold its less bloody side up over the water for Hakan to take a photo. *Just one photo*, brothers and sisters, of this fish I had wanted to catch for over half a century—and . . . well, what can I tell you but the truth? The tigerfish gave a mighty thrash and wrenched the BogaGrip out of my hand.

I stood on the stern seat and watched the dying fish, still attached to the BogaGrip, being carried by it, struggling, toward the bottom: a vision I wouldn't wish on my worst enemy. I wondered if my father had had moments like this far away from home. If he had, I believed I knew what he would have made of them.

Oh well, I thought: There is still the noble mahseer of India.

17

RIVERS OWNED IN THE MIND

My friend Hughie MacDowell and I took a break from fishing around noon and sat on the river's bank for a sandwich and a few pulls of Glenfiddich from the silver hip flask his wife, Knuckles, had given him. I couldn't remember ever in my life being happier.

This was in April of 1986. It was my second month-long trip to the trouting moveable feast that is New Zealand and my first visit to the Ngaruroro River, a thirty-minute helicopter flight from Turangi back into the sublime backcountry of the Kaimanawa mountains of the North Island. I had just cast a #14 Adams to an eight-pound-plus rainbow who ate the fly and promptly broke me off behind a rock. The Ngaruroro (it is pronounced nigh-ru-roara, a sound like waves on a beach) seemed to be a necklace of emeralds separated by diamonds—a thing of ineffable worth that filled you while you were on it with a buoyant and radiant well-being. I had fallen in love with almost every river I had met thus far in New Zealand, but I adored this one. I said so to Hughie and he smiled. Hughie was then a nonpareil trout angler, guide, and fly tier, with a trenchant Irish wit and a poet's soul. On that April day he and I were both drifting a stretch of quiet water in our lives, but just around the corner were some howling Class VI rapids that would spit us out separately a few years later, still afloat but in serious need of the kind of solace Hughie spoke of then after the smile. He tapped his temple and said: "You know, I own this river in my mind. And whenever I'm in, say, a bus station in Los Angeles, all I have to do is say its name and everything is fine."

Both before and after that day with Hughie, I have had occasion to fall in love with other rivers. Some—like the Test in Hampshire, the Jardine in Northern Australia, the Nolichucky in the Smoky Mountains, the Eg in Mongolia, the Hatiguanico in Cuba, the Grimsa in Iceland, the Segre in the Spanish Pyrenees—were unforgettable flings. With Argentina's Traful and Quebec's Bonaventure, Bruce's Spring Creek on the South Island, the Zolotaya on the Kola Peninsula and others, there have been long affairs. And then there are a few, along with the Ngaruroro, that have gone from my heart into my mind and live there, summonable to rustling life whenever I call them up.

Though there are countless lakes and flats, shorelines and oceans that I am devoted to, none of them inhabits me the way these rivers do. Wondering at this moment why that is, it seems to me because it is in the flow of rivers that fishing most fully becomes the act of self-emptying that, for me, gives it its most meaningful and durable resonance. If intruding yourself into the eating habits of pea-brained creatures with fins is—as my wife, for one, suspects—a pastime for dull-normals, it is also one easily flogged into a sort of sublime obsession by the saintly eagerness to unite yourself with something only blind belief can assure you exists. What is called patience in fishing is really just the ongoing belief that the next entreaty you cast into the void (or the one after that, or the next) will connect you to the two thousand-pound black marlin, the five-foot Atlantic salmon, the ten-pound farm pond bass of your dreams. That is why, for many of us, the nut of the thing is that moment when the fly stops, before the line begins to rise: the moment, perhaps not unlike our last, of being tight to something unmanifest, but imminently about to be.

I would aver that those moments are what keep coots like myself stringing up rods year after year in out-of-the-way places long after the urgings of blood-lust, competition, and hang-it-on-the-wall frenzy have subsided. In fact, it is the very absence of those demands, in the poof! disappearance of one's self, that best defines such moments, and that can make one's angling in them seem sacerdotal. For me, this flushing out of the stridencies of self-awareness, and the subliminal, soul-feeding connections that flushing out engenders, happens most often amid the phantasmagoria of rivers. And on a few of those, it has happened so fully and vividly for me, that, like Hughie McDowell, I can conjure myself

out of any old Los Angeles bus station I find myself in simply by speaking their names.

My sons, Latham and Shelby, then twelve and seven, and I are in my green canoe *The Recruitment*, named for a magazine short story that paid for it. It is a late summer afternoon nearly forty years ago. We have put in the Blackwater River below Webster, New Hampshire, and are floating to the bridge by the Popes' house in Hopkinton. In the bow, Latham is using my father's old Abercrombie & Fitch glass fly rod to drop a big yellow popper up close to the bushy bank and into the fishy-looking pockets made by branches of trees that have fallen into the river. Shelby sits on the carrying thwart, flipping a Rapala, and I paddle in the stern, easing the canoe around the slow, snaking meanders of the exquisite little river. Its banks are only thirty feet apart in places, its water the color of espresso; and each turn opens a new, small tableau—turtles on a log, a pair of wood ducks exploding off the water—and a new picture-perfect smallmouth hole.

There may be, somewhere, a lovelier woodland smallmouth river than the Blackwater, but I have not met it. It is a petite, raven-haired vamp of bottomless eyes and few words, who can sulk one day when a three-hour float might produce four or five fish on the top (where we always fish) and stand your hair on end the next—on a day like today.

Shelby is fighting a three-pound smallmouth up to the gunwale, the ultralight spinning rod bowed almost into a full circle. As I lean over to lip the fish, I see a bigger one porpoise and crash Latham's popper, its thick, furrowing back black and bronze. We will release a dozen and keep two for supper before the bridge in Hopkinton, and we will never, in five years of floating the river, see another person fishing it.

The river I hope runs through it for me on the other side will look something like the two-and-a-half-mile stretch of the Ruby near Alder, Montana, that belonged to my friends Craig and Martha Woodson: dainty and purling, its banks a manicured comeliness of cottonwoods, its amber water dimpled with brown-trout rises. And those browns are some of the feistiest and most agreeable anywhere: beautifully colored, acrobatic, quick-to-take fish that are found exactly where they are supposed to be in a river's textbook runs, seams, and pools.

The Ruby is a river to make you feel like Izaak Walton—a wet-wading and bank-fishing river that invites long, meditative breaks for reverie, a pipe, good conversation. It is also a river that can toss out epiphanies like flowers from a basket.

My young friends Ethan and Jason have their first day of trout fishing just under their belts. Yesterday they floated a hot stretch of the Madison, lobbing nymphs under indicators into runs beside the boat and letting them float there until their guide told them to strike. They caught lots of fish that way and decided they were naturals at the trout fishing game. Today we are on the Woodson's Ruby—a different kettle of fish. I walk the banks with them, looking for rises, and then they take turns blowing the fish. They can't reach it or line it, they drag over it, they hook willows and each other. But the Ruby is, as ever, openhearted and generous, and maybe even a little smitten with my boys. First one then the other finally gets everything right, releases his first dry-fly trout, and looks up at me from knee-deep in the Ruby with a fresh, thrilled, lifetime scar of comprehension on his face.

Midway through our second morning at Jack Cooper's Minipi Camp in Labrador, our guide, Rol Burry, ran Perry Munro and me by boat all the way down the lake to a little river running between Minipi and Anne Marie Lakes and named for the latter. It was late August. Rol thought the spawners might be well up the river and no one had been there for over a year. It might be good, he said. If it was not, all we would have wasted would be an afternoon, and he believed Perry and I would like the river.

We ate lunch at the outlet pool of the Anne Marie, then started rock-hopping upstream under a hot sun. The river was ice-clear, cold, and fast, with needle-nosed spruces crowding its banks. We saw wolf tracks and fresh moose droppings, and the utter wildness of the place felt like testing the blade of a sharp knife against your thumb. In every pool were brook trout in their metaphysically beautiful rust, cream, and olive spawning colors. Perry and I leap-frogged each other from pool to pool, casting big, barbless Mud-dlers. After only two or three pools we began to wonder out loud among the laughter and shouting if this would ruin us for any fishing ever, anywhere again.

We didn't leave the Anne Marie until nine that night for the hour and a half moonlit run back to camp, and leaving then was a wrench for me that bordered on panic. We had fished maybe three or four miles up the river, about half its length. In my note-book I had recorded what we caught, knowing it was a catch I would not want to be inexact about: sixty to seventy-five fish of a pound and under; fourteen between one and three pounds; and eleven glorious brookies over three—including two over seven, and five more over five.

On our hurried scramble back downstream to the boat, Rol said that as far as he knew no one had ever fished all the way up to Anne Marie Lake, and he let that thought hang in the darkening air.

We called it *la vie de truite*—jumping into the freezing, muscular current and letting it carry us downstream to whatever sandbar we had pulled into to camp for the night. Jerome Gary and "Spinnerbait" Carlson and I would participate in this trout's life every evening after we had built a fire we could run back to, submerging ourselves in the glacial blue Mulchatna and facing upstream while we were whipped downriver. We almost lost Spinnerbait like that one night—and had to go retrieve him in one of the four rafts in which the eight of us were presumptuously floating that grizzly-wild, killer-beauty of a river—but the ritual seemed to make more comprehensible the outsized, preternaturally fit rainbows we were catching all day.

It was supposed to be a guided trip, but wasn't. The wine, the rib eyes, the lobster tails had gone missing, along with more basic items such as bread and lettuce. But we had about forty pounds of moose jerky and the fish we caught. We had maybe the only six straight days of clear, warm, windless weather in Alaskan history, exhilarating company, *la vie de truite*, and the experience of the river itself, which was pushed from being just attention worthy into riveting by the outfitter having forgotten the maps along with the mayo, and by our having only a vague idea of where we would have to meet the float planes that would carry us out.

I have never concentrated on a river so hard and for so long. Right now, in a writing shack in Nova Scotia, I can see the Mulchatna's bodybuilder curves, its giant, pale rainbows, the grizzly tracks in the sand at one of our campsites, the eagles feeding on rotten sockeyes. And I can see to this day, as if I had been caught there and later released, the chill, blue, hazardous rush of its current over my open eyes.

Now as much home water to me as the Blackwater once was, Nova Scotia's Margaree is a river that escapes the forest to flow though widening, sunlit pasturelands and meadows on its way to the sea. And I believe I love the river as passionately as I do partially because I feel associated with it in that escape—sunnier, more exposed, and closer to the sea myself than I was on the Blackwater.

I also love it because it was my dues-paying river in salmon fishing. No form of fly fishing is more difficult to do well or looks easier than that for Atlantic salmon—the things the real experts do differently than you being hidden, or at least hard to identify, until you are one of them. My cherry day at it was on the Margaree over forty years ago. I bought a few flies at a convenience store, waded into that flirting little hussy, and expected my first salmon within ten casts.

In fact, my first salmon from the Margaree came well over ten thousand casts and almost a decade later. Over that time the river gave me the gate in every way imaginable. But it always did so like Katherine Hepburn turning down Spencer Tracy for a date early into one of their movies—firmly, but leaving the door open for later with a wink. Like Spencer, I kept coming back, and the first time I finally scored on the Margaree, with a bright hen fish of about eight pounds, is one of the river moments I summon most often.

Since that moment I have had affairs with more than a seemly number of salmon rivers here and there, but it is the Margaree I always come home to. She is more beautiful to me than ever now, with her gay, skirt-gathering pace, her meadow pools, the way she stretches like a cat just before the sea. She is far more generous to me too these days. And yet every fish I catch there is one I'd like to tell Hughie McDowell about, sitting together on the bank of the Ngaruroro or some other river owned in the mind.

ACKNOWLEDGMENTS

The author would like to thank the following magazines for sponsoring much of the gallivanting recorded in this volume: *Garden & Gun*, *Forbes Life*, *Men's Journal*, and *Sports Afield*. Also, thanks to Jake MacDonald, in whose fine anthology, *Casting Quiet Waters*, one of the stories here first appeared. No amount of thanks can convey my gratitude to John Swan—splendid artist and fishing pal—for the artwork he contributed to this book. And finally, my thanks to Tom Montgomery, who is featured often in these pages: nonpareil photographer, sportsman, traveling companion, and friend.

ABOUT THE AUTHOR

Charles Gaines is the author of the National Book Award finalist novel *Stay Hungry* and the international nonfiction bestseller *Pumping Iron*, along with more than twenty other books. His articles and stories have appeared in *Harper's*, *Sports Illustrated*, *Audubon*, *Forbes Life*, *Town & Country*, *Architectural Digest*, *Esquire*, *Men's Journal*, *Playboy*, *Garden and Gun*, *Sports Afield*, *Field & Stream*, and other magazines. He has also received two Emmy Awards for his television writing, and has written the scripts for a number of produced feature and feature-documentary films. A lifelong sportsman and outdoor adventurer, Gaines has been a dedicated wing shooter and bird-dog trainer, a rock and ice climber, a ski instructor and winter mountaineer, a whitewater canoeist, small-boat sailor, and certified diver. He also co-invented the game of paintball. But his favorite outdoor activity has always been fly fishing, at which he has had the great good fortune to flail away in over twenty-five countries. He serves as a US director of the Atlantic Salmon Federation, and is a founding board member of the US Fly Fishing Team. He lives with his wife, Patricia, in Nova Scotia and Alabama.